ROARING LION

To

Bart and Margaret

In

appreciation

R. L. Peterson

By the same author
STORM OVER BORNEO

ROARING LION

*Vital turning point in Chinese church
growth in Indonesian Borneo*

by

ROBERT PETERSON

LONDON

OVERSEAS MISSIONARY FELLOWSHIP

S. U.
CHRISTIAN BOOK CENTRE
36-H, PRINSEP STREET,
SINGAPORE, 7.

© OVERSEAS MISSIONARY FELLOWSHIP

First published	..	..	*September 1968*
Reprinted	..	..	..	*January 1969*
Reprinted	..	..	..	*June 1969*
Reprinted	..	..	..	*March 1970*
Reprinted	..	..	..	*May 1971*

SBN 85363 069 0

Made in Great Britain
Published by Overseas Missionary Fellowship,
Newington Green, London N16 9QD
and printed by The Camelot Press Ltd., London and Southampton

CONTENTS

HISTORICAL INTRODUCTION

First Chinese in Borneo

Long before Columbus sailed into the New World thousands of Chinese migrated south to a new home in Borneo (now known as Kalimantan) and, for nearly a thousand years, generations lived and died knowing nothing of the Lion of Judah, but were slaves to another who roared and devoured at will. To the religion of their fathers they added many customs and practices common to the animistic tribes of the islands. Spiritism and demon worship occupied a major place in their daily lives and "the prince of the power of the air" boldly manifested his unchallenged dominion over them.

Earliest Christian witness

The earliest records of any Christian witness among the Chinese in West Kalimantan show that among more recent immigrants were Christians from the coastal areas of South China. Before 1916 meeting places were set apart for worship in the towns of Pontianak and Singkawang, as well as in one or two other coastal villages, and missionaries from the West trekked through jungle areas with the Gospel message. In 1951, when a new chapter began, there were two congregations struggling to remain alive, but making little, if any, impact for the Lord among the quarter of a million Chinese scattered in every city, town and village in West Kalimantan. The community was sharply divided politically with more than half giving support to the then new Peking Government, and even among the church leaders were found those who gave political allegiance to New China. Being traders and financiers, few had any time for spiritual things and showed little interest in the Gospel. On the other hand, old and young, rich and poor, they lived all their lifetime subject to bondage, slaves to Satan and his emissaries, and in constant fear of evil spirits which were as real to them as the wealth they possessed.

A new beginning

After 1945 the Gospel message lost any appeal it may have had, and the missionary was considered an imperialist intruder. Gospel tracts were not read and, in general, it seemed that "the god of this world" had complete control over these his subjects. Well-meaning observers assured us it was impossible to expect any spiritual results working under such conditions and, for the space of four to five years after the Overseas Missionary Fellowship began work in 1952, they seemed right. However, something began to happen and, in the next few short years, more than 1,500 men and women came into a personal saving experience of the grace of God. Political barriers were broken down; hearts hardened by years of rejecting the Gospel were melted; lives which had been wholly given over to serving the Devil were made new and surrendered to the Lord for willing service. Young people joined together to form evangelistic bands and responded to urgent invitations to come and bring the Gospel to country villages. Other young people dedicated their lives for full-time service and sought training in Bible schools and colleges. Some have gone to other islands as home missionaries. One young couple has recently responded to a call from Holland to go and evangelize Chinese living there.

The invincible Church

By mid-1967 more than twenty churches had been organized and regular worship services were being held in twenty-six centres. Eight church buildings had been completed and others were in the process of construction. But, you ask, when did the break come? What could be the explanation for such a change among the materialistic, spirit-worshipping Chinese in West Kalimantan? What made this dark area become one of the bright spots of missionary work in recent years? We do not overlook the years of preparation and patient, faithful seed-sowing, or the watering of the seed by the faithful prayers of saints around the world; but *we believe it is not just coincidental that when the Lord's servants commenced openly to challenge the power of darkness and, in the name of our victorious Lord, command the demons to come out of the possessed ones, the gates of hell began to yield and captives were set free.* The following chapters record a few of the personal experiences of those deeply involved, those who challenged Satan and who were challenged by him. These are not a few isolated experiences of one or two missionaries, but similar things have been witnessed by each of the workers in that area. When the power of the Gospel was proclaimed and confirmed by miracles of deliverance from Satan's power, other men and women began to seek freedom from their bondage and deliverance from the power of Satan. Believers were encouraged to exercise the authority over evil spirits promised them by the Lord Himself, and the Gospel became a living reality, not just another religion.

Counter-attack

The Enemy did not yield easily and many have been his counter-attacks. During the closing months of 1967 he stirred up evil men among the Dyaks who, by a blood covenant, yielded themselves soul and body to the task of destroying a segment of the population of West Kalimantan. Approximately 50,000 residents of Chinese descent left everything and fled to the coastal towns to protect their lives. Some did not escape and were slaughtered. While ten congregations have been scattered and hundreds of Chinese believers have sought refuge in coastal cities, the "Roaring Lion" has once again overstepped himself. This unprecedented concentration of Chinese from the remote and inaccessible jungle areas has opened a new chapter in the story of the Lord's work in West Kalimantan. This concentration makes it entirely possible to bring the Gospel to those otherwise unreached ones, and the churches are taking the opportunity to do so. The lion continues to roar only because he knows his time is short.

GEORGE M. STEED

OMF Superintendent
in Indonesia.

FOREWORD

AS A MISSIONARY in Burma I have had experience of the power and activity of the forces of darkness, though now I could wish I had been better instructed and more spiritually fit to deal with them.

Of late I have also seen something of the dire effects of demonic activity in Ethiopia and in England. Quite unsought, the Lord has brought me into direct confrontation more recently with the activities of evil spirits in the home country, and my eyes have been opened as never before to see how real is their work even in Christians. For this reason I have welcomed the opportunity to read the manuscript of *Roaring Lion* and gladly accept the invitation to write this Foreword. I do it in the strong conviction that not only is the record of the activities of the spirits of wickedness recounted here absolutely authentic, but that the manner of dealing with them has been the only one possible.

I pray God that this little book may have a wide circulation and that He will use it to help many of His people to realize that here we have no tale of "superstitious humbug", but rather a sober account of dreadful and devastating realities. "We wrestle not against flesh and blood, but against principalities . . . against the rulers of the darkness of this world . . ." (Eph. 6.12); but the sad fact is that so many Christians as yet know little of this warfare and, until we take steps to right this failure, we shall continue to grope in the dark and remain helpless in face of the rapid advance of Satanic forces in these last days.

As Mr. Peterson so rightly emphasizes in the last chapter, our strength lies in the Victor of Calvary who is seated at the right hand of God, far above all principality and power. We share His authority who said: "All authority in heaven and on earth has been given to me. Go then . . . I am with you all the days to the close of the age" (Matt. 28.18–20, *Amplified Bible*).

Putting our trust in His total victory on Calvary's cross, we must enthrone Christ as Lord in every part of our life. Then, encased in the whole armour of God, we shall be able effectively to do battle with the hosts of darkness and see the deliverance of many precious souls now literally held by them helpless captives. Let us therefore be willing to face the ugly reality of Satan and his emissaries, and go forward in the Name of Jesus and in the power of His Holy Spirit to pray, to resist, to stand and see the salvation of the Lord.

T. R. V. GURNEY, M.B., Ch.B.

British Home Secretary,
Red Sea Mission Team.

AUTHOR'S PREFACE

"IT IS NOTHING but hallucination, fantastic dreams if you please," were the words ringing in my ears long after I had heard them. I had just come from the land of Borneo and was relating some of my personal experiences in dealing with demon activity. I was prepared for a lack of understanding in these matters, but was little prepared for a complete "refutation" of all I had witnessed and seen. I felt then as I feel now that no one can refute one's personal experiences. They can explain them away, but not disprove them. I have since spent much time in the study of this subject and the Bible was and is my main textbook in explaining these experiences.

Knowing demonic activity from experience is important, for this affords much confirmation of the inspiration of Scripture. I feel also that personal experience, to be valid in a study like this, must be interpreted in the light of the Word of God. This I have sought to do.

The Old Testament deals with demonic activity in many of its aspects. Christ regarded demonism as a stern reality. The writers of the Epistles spared not in their exposure of these evil forces. Today we see the foolish heart of man darkened by the ceaseless activity of this host of seducing spirits. Can we in all honesty then, let the "hallucination" statement above go by without challenge? I think not! I have therefore endeavoured to write what I have personally witnessed of demon activity and have sought to explain it in the light of Holy Writ.

My prayer is that this book will help the Christian to know a little better the "depths of Satan" and by knowing, to help him "fight the good fight of faith".

CHAPTER ONE

DARKEST OF THE DARK

"Who hath delivered us from the POWER OF DARKNESS, and hath translated us into the kingdom of his dear Son" (Col. 1.13).

SHORTLY AFTER Chinese New Year and at the Festival of the First Full Moon after New Year, the Chinese in West Borneo devote several days to the worship of evil spirits. To the uninitiated, the new missionary included, this time can be of great wonderment. Young and old alike build intricate facsimiles of birds, four-footed beasts, and creeping things (see Rom. 1.22, 23). These things are very beautiful to the eye and it is easy to be infected with the spirit of the occasion. Communities vie with each other over the best-made dragons. The history of these dragons is wrapped up in Chinese religious traditions. Teams of young men are chosen to carry the dragon through the streets, dancing to the beat of drums and gongs. Practice begins days before the festival, and only when the priests are satisfied with their performance are the teams allowed to take part in the ceremonies.

On the day, the dragons are taken to the temples where priests pronounce a blessing on them. Then they are allowed to go into the streets to begin the festivities. The people actually worship these "blessed dragons" which dance in and out of the homes where the people bow to them and present their offerings. Thus the coffers of the priests are enriched. The beautifully constructed birds are also objects of worship.

Every Chinese community in this land has its order of priests and sorcerers, each of whom has a duty to perform in the idolatrous ceremonies. From among these priests, some are chosen to perform acts of self-laceration under the influence of evil spirits. The priests sit in specially made chairs, the parts in contact with the body being made out of spikes and knives. I found these knives as sharp as razor blades and could detect no sham in the whole performance. The priest chosen for the ceremony is first prepared by the worship of demons and a deliberate invitation for the demon to possess the body. As the demon enters an immediate change is noticed: the eyes become glazed and the possessed man dances about with such a light step that he seems to have overcome the power of gravity. His words emanate, not from the vocal chords, but from the pit of the stomach and he may issue commands to another attendant priest in a language not his own and even one that he cannot normally speak at all.

When the demon's wishes have been fulfilled (for the demon is now in control), knives, daggers or sharpened bamboo sticks are handed to the man. I have witnessed these instruments being thrust through the cheeks, the tongue, and sometimes through vital organs of the body without a trace of bleeding or feeling of pain. The demon-possessed man jumps about waving a large sword in the air and then, with a mighty leap, seats himself on the chair on which he is carried about the town as an object of worship. This goes on all day as visits are paid to a number of temples where the man is worshipped and adored as a god of the miraculous. The heathen acknowledge the presence of evil spirits but because of their miraculous powers they fear and worship them. Not to do so would invite sickness or even death.

It was in just this sort of atmosphere that I found myself early in my missionary career. The senior missionary had gone on holiday and I, with my limited language, had no one to turn to for advice. The few Christians, aware of the danger, shut themselves in their homes and stayed there throughout the festivities. I should have followed their example, but instead I unthinkingly set forth with my camera and thus walked right into the hornet's nest. So anxious was I to see the spectacle and to get a photographic record that I omitted to pray before setting out, an omission which doubtless contributed to the overwhelming darkness so soon to overtake me.

The crowds were enormous and jostled for the best view-points. For days trucks, jeeps and buses had been bringing them in from outlying places until there was hardly a place to stand. Singkawang, a city of 40,000, was now swarming with over 100,000 people. I had no trouble in winding my way through the crowd. Partly because of my race, but more likely because of my bulk, I found people making way for me. I soon found the best place of vantage for taking pictures, and before the parade passed, I had an excellent opportunity to study the faces and the dress of the onlookers. It was interesting, to say the least. Old and young were dressed in their holiday best, the Malay women in colourful *sarongs* and blouses and the Chinese women in pyjama-style suits. Many Indonesians though not idolaters, being Muslims, were nevertheless attracted by the excitement.

Suddenly the sound of drums and gongs announced the approach of the procession. On this occasion thirteen different communities and temples were represented, each with its dragon, unicorn and demon possessed priest. Of the thirteen priests carried in the special chairs, only one was a woman and she alone had no stiletto penetrating her face and body. As the parade drew nearer I felt as if I were shut up in some dark prison with no way of escape. I tried to reassure myself that nothing could harm me. Despite an acute sense of impending danger, I disregarded it and began to take pictures.

When the procession was about halfway through, I felt an irresistible urge to go closer to take a picture of one of the evil-looking priests. I had no sooner pressed through the crowd when, with a roar of rage, the priest jumped down from his chair and rushed towards me with his sword lifted high. In the few moments before he reached me, I had ample opportunity to look into his eyes which fascinated me and semi-hypnotized me. All the evil in the world seemed to be in the eyes of that possessed man. A great horror of darkness came upon me. I was so afraid that I could not move, let alone call for help. When the sword had almost touched my throat, my knees buckled just enough so that the sword missed its mark.

Although it was the crowds that saved me, it was in fact the Lord who stayed the hand of the Enemy, despite the fact that I felt deserted by all, including God. For Satan blinds and confuses the minds of those who walk in disobedience to God's Word! In the excitement the crowd hemmed me in and the priest was unable to make a second pass at me. Thoroughly terrified, I got away as quickly as I could. Safely home, I spent two of the most terrible hours of my life, hours that were darkest of the dark!

In my fear I shut all the doors and windows of the house and barred them. I even shoved chairs against the doors, though this was a futile barrier against the "powers of darkness". I paced up and down with no voice to cry to God for mercy. It seemed that God had shut the door into His presence in my face and no amount of effort could open it. How masterful are the lies of Satan and how unmerciful he is as he deceives God's children! The Lord Jesus called him a liar (John 8.44) and he has been lying ever since.

Unable to pray, I reached the brink of despair, and an overwhelming desire to do away with my life came over me, and for two hours I fought suggestions of suicide.

At this very moment the Holy Spirit was moving two people to pray for me, one in the United States and the other in Canada. They both at the very same time had the impression that I was in some impending danger, and poured out their hearts to God for my deliverance. It was only weeks after that we found out how God had used them to disperse my cloud of darkness.

My release was instantaneous. It was just as if I had been groping my way through a fog bank for two hours when suddenly I emerged into sunshine. I threw myself on to the bed and cried out to God for forgiveness. Joy filled my soul and all my fear was banished. The promise "greater is he that is in you, than he that is in the world" (I John 4.4) came to mind. Later I went out again, but this time not with bravado, but forearmed with prayer and carrying a handful of tracts, I went forth, in the confidence that victory over the Enemy is the Lord's and He is on our side.

When did I give place to the "powers of darkness" and allow them to get a hold of me? I could not plead innocence or lack of experience as an excuse, for I had been warned during Bible and missionary training: "What concord hath Christ with Belial? Or what part hath he that believeth with an infidel?" (II Cor. 6.15). The Christian is not instructed to live an ascetic life, for how then could he witness to the unbeliever? We are told, however, to walk "not in the counsel of the ungodly, nor (stand) in the way of sinners, nor (sit) in the seat of the scornful" (Ps. 1.1). When the Christian fails to heed this exhortation he forfeits the blessing of God and leaves himself open to his "adversary the devil (who) as a roaring lion, walketh about, seeking whom he may devour" (I Pet. 5.8). It was a wrong motive that brought about my bout with the forces of evil. I went out to see the sights and to take pictures, with no thought of witnessing while doing so. I did not even pray before stepping into Satan's territory. In other words I was playing with fire and I got burned. Except for the purpose of undertaking some service for the Lord, we are warned to steer clear of anything pertaining to idolatry. "The things which the Gentiles sacrifice, they sacrifice to devils, and not to God: and I would not that ye should have fellowship with devils" (I Cor. 10.20). Every Christian who disobeys this warning leaves himself open to the snares of the Devil (I Tim. 3.7), however strong a Christian he may be. "Wherefore, let him that thinketh he standeth take heed lest he fall" (I Cor. 10.12). While we do not need to think there is a devil behind every bush, we do need to heed the biblical warning.

My experience does not stand alone in this battle with "powers of darkness" in West Borneo. In over ten years of ministry here, I have encountered many Christians broken, discouraged and defeated because they failed to heed God's warnings. Among them is David Bong.

This young man with over seven years in the Christian faith had ample opportunity to study God's teaching regarding the dangerous, occult powers so prevalent here. This man was actually attending a Short Term Bible School when he became entrapped in Satan's web. On the very day that he fell into the snare a warning had been given at chapel on the verse, "(Walk) not in the counsel of the ungodly". But David listened to the counsel of the ungodly who invited him to go to the Mid-year Festival to see the sights. He sinned knowingly in agreeing to go, played truant from the school, and went to this festival notorious for its virulent, idolatrous atmosphere.

Returning home he began to have violent body tremors, heard taunting voices out of the darkness that brought abject fear to his soul. He feared he was losing his mind, when he had no power to resist the voices. They urged him to behave in an anti-social way and even said,

"You may as well do away with your life, for it's lost anyway!"

The young wife heard no voices, but noticing her

husband's strange contortions, she rushed for help. When several Christians arrived, David was violently sick and each time they tried to talk or pray with him, he vomited. So their only recourse was to retire to the church for united prayer. Praise God, deliverance came. David confessed his sin, and is a warning to other Christians to "come out from among them, and be ye separate, saith the Lord, and touch not the unclean thing" (II Cor. 6.17). And this we believe includes many things besides the open worship of idols.

The psychiatrist might explain the reaction of David to his experience as a "guilt complex"; and the medical doctor would probably say that the body tremors were just an attack of malaria. But not all such cases can easily be explained on medical or psychological grounds. The Bible is our most reliable commentary on the Christian's disobedience to God's specific commands and throws light on the impact of the unseen world on the seen. If this is accepted, it paves the way for the inspired teaching on the subject.

Dr. Merrill Unger says, "No one choosing light can be invaded by the forces of darkness. It is only as the enlightened will deliberately chooses darkness, or yields to sin, that it exposes itself to demonic power."[1] Mrs. Penn-Lewis tells us that believers are open to attacks by evil spirits "because they have in most cases unwittingly fulfilled the conditions upon which evil spirits work. Such attacks are the outcome of yielding to sins of the flesh, or any sin which gives evil spirits a hold in the fallen nature."[2]

[1] *Biblical Demonology* (Merrill F. Unger), p. 27.
[2] *War on the Saints* (Mrs. Penn-Lewis), 6th ed., pp. 68–69.

Rev. J. A. MacMillan says, "It is a truth not always realized that any wilful sin invites every other sin, and when some sin has been yielded to carelessly or thoughtlessly the sinner may find himself a little later beset with temptation that he may have thought had no appeal to him. Thus when conscience is disobeyed, and known sin wilfully given access to the mind and heart, the protection of truth is weakened or withdrawn and some spirit of evil may gain lodgment."[1]

I believe the urge to commit suicide can be understood by Bible teaching, as well as by experience. Consider John 8.44, "He was a murderer from the beginning"; I Pet. 5.8 (*Living Letters*), "Be careful, watch out for attacks from Satan, your great enemy. He prowls around like a hungry, roaring lion for some victim to tear apart." After King Saul sinned, the Spirit of the Lord departed from him, with Scripture recording that, until his death by suicide, he was plagued by an "evil spirit" (I Sam. 16.14, 31.4). When Luke wrote that "Satan entered into Judas" (22.3), it is implied that the dynamic of his suicide was Satanic. The Gospels speak of demons vexing their victims to the point of suicide (Matt. 17.15–18, Mark 9.18). It need not be assumed, however, that all suicidal impulses are directly Satanic.

Only two experiences relating to the suicidal impulse are recorded in this chapter. But in chapter 8 a case is cited where a demon brought about the suicidal death of several teen-age girls. Recently in one of our centres a young wife by the name of Mrs. Li committed suicide. For over two years previously

[1] *Modern Demon Possession* (Rev. J. A. MacMillan), pp. 26–27.

she had shown every evidence of being a happy, well-balanced Christian, but gradually she became despondent over not being able to bear children. Finally she took poison after, by her own confession, listening to "inner voices".

This is no isolated case. Dr. Unger says: "Self-destruction seems far better explained, at least in the majority of cases, by demonic influence or possession than by insanity."[1]

Without being dogmatic, it is just possible that the high rate of suicide today is due to the work of Satan and his servants, the demons. One sometimes hears it said, "I am a Christian, so the Devil cannot touch me." With this, Scripture does not agree, and many no longer follow the Lord because they underrated Satan's power. "Ye did run well: who did hinder you that ye should not obey the truth?" (Gal. 5.7) comes as a salutary warning to us all.

[1] *Biblical Demonology*, p. 40.

CHAPTER TWO

HOUSE OF FEAR

". . . Them which were vexed with unclean spirits" (Acts 5.16).

"NO SELF-RESPECTING GOAT would live in it", were the words of the Assistant Director of the Overseas Missionary Fellowship in describing the house we were to live in for two years. To a young couple just launched on their first pioneer missionary effort, these words were no deterrent. A nail, a new roof tile, some paint, and a picture or two made a remarkable change in the so-called "goat house". A house is not a home until there are people living in it. This particular house had been vacant for several years for reasons unknown to us at the time.

One thing is sure, however, that the time spent in the house was one of great blessing.[1] Our hearts were thrilled to see a number turn "to God from idols to serve the living and true God" (I Thess. 1.9). These converts became the nucleus of the young church, the first for many a long year to be established among the Chinese in West Borneo. We felt that this infant church needed the entire building and we tried, therefore, to find another house for ourselves but unsuccessfully. When our son was born, our joy was tempered with anxiety. Besides being very small, the house was built over a canal and there would be no easy way of protecting him later on from the danger of falling into

[1] *Borneo Breakthrough* (Sylvia Houliston).

the water. We could not understand God's seeming deafness to our entreaties until we discovered the history of the house. Then we knew why God kept us there.

Months after arrival we were told of the stir we made among the villagers as they excitedly awaited what they believed would be the dire results from living in this house. "Don't they know that the 'god' of the bridge dwells there?" "Didn't the last family to live in that house lose four of their children to this 'god'?" "We would never dare to live in it! Let it rot!" "What audacity of these foreigners to challenge our god!"

They believed this so-called "god of the bridge" made its domicile in our home by the river. The fear of this god or demon was pathetically real, for if the worshippers relaxed in their worship, the demon would strike with vengeance. Several people who had failed to bring incense to burn under a trestle of the bridge at the appointed time suffered sickness or death, and no one questioned why several children had died in the home one after another when the occupants defied the "god" and refused to worship because of their Communist beliefs. Whether death was natural or violent, all believed the dynamic force behind it to be this "god of the bridge".

Satan spares no effort in his desire for worship. He even sought the worship of the Lord Jesus Christ: "If thou therefore wilt worship me, all shall be thine" (Luke 4.7). The master passion of Satan for worship leads him to gain worship by whatever method brings the best results. He gains the worship of millions of

26

intelligent people through counterfeit systems of truth, persuading them he does not exist; or that he holds no dread for the educated and informed, who either belittle his influence or dismiss it as humbug. The superstitious, on the other hand, are held in bondage by fear, a fear the Western world cannot understand because it defies explanation! Even after living fourteen years among superstitious people I still cannot explain it rationally, but I just know it exists.

This fear of evil spirits is real and the writer of the book of Hebrews speaks of those "who through fear of death were all their lifetime subject to bondage" (Heb. 2.15). It is an unshaken belief among the heathen in West Borneo that death comes from the power of an unseen spirit. Village after village has its vacant house believed to be occupied by spirits. "Why tempt your fate by living in such a house?" they say. It is this fear that the spirits can cause sickness and death that drives people on in their worship of spirits and their desire to placate them.

The Word of God tells us Satan is a murderer: "Since we, God's children, are human beings—made of flesh and blood—He became flesh and blood too by being born in human form; for only as a human being could He die and in dying destroy the devil *who has the power of death*" (Heb. 2.14, *Living Letters*). Scripture also illustrates how Satan can cause sickness: "So went Satan forth from the presence of the Lord, and smote Job with sore boils . . ." (Job 2.7). If we accept the Scriptural teaching about Satan, it should not be difficult to believe that there is good reason for fear among those who have had experience of his power for so long.

Was that why our neighbours held their breath when we moved into this "house of fear"? They believed the place to be a god-domain. As people gradually opened their hearts to us, revealing their fears, we came to believe that God in His wisdom had kept us living in the house until the town was convinced that their "gods" had no power over us. How precious is the truth of the Word of God! "Ye are of God, little children, and have overcome them: because greater is he that is in you, than he (Satan) that is in the world" (I John 4.4).

It is difficult for some to accept the belief that a house can be the domicile of unseen spirits, even though the "haunted house" phenomenon is fairly common. Some of the difficulty lies in the unwillingness to admit in this age that there are such beings as demons. Many are ignorant of "the depths of Satan" (Rev. 2.24), and dismiss the concept of demons as pure mediaeval superstition. The Scriptures, however, provide overwhelming evidence of the existence of a personal Devil and his minions, the demons. To deny their existence or laugh at the idea is in itself to suffer from a blindness brought about by Satan, "the god of this world" (II Cor. 4.4).

We ourselves were never conscious of our house being the domain of evil spirits. On the contrary we have every reason to believe that the moment we entered the door the demons fled, for, as children of light, God has "delivered us from the power of darkness" (Col. 1.13). While the Jewish exorcists who tried to drive out evil spirits in the name of the Lord Jesus were overcome by them (Acts 19.13–17), true believers whose hearts are right find that the demons fear and flee from their presence. Our foe is a vanquished foe and victory is assured because of Christ in us (I John 4.4).

"Why," we may ask, "was this house the dwelling place of demons? Were there not many houses from which they could have chosen? Why then select this particular one?" Research into the history of the house revealed that it had been a hotbed of idolatrous activity in earlier years, and idolatry appears to be the tool of demons. Through idolatry they gain the worship they crave.

The Old Testament reveals that idolatry is closely allied with demons. People bow down to an image in worship, but the real personalities behind the idols are demons. "For all the gods of the nations are idols . . ." (Ps. 96.5). The Apostle Paul confirms this when he says: ". . . the things which the Gentiles sacrifice, they sacrifice to devils, and not to God" (I Cor. 10.20). Mrs. Needham declares "The root offence of idolatry was demonology. All its stupidity and senseless ceremony were but addenda to the main facts. The senses were gratified, the passions unloosed, the conscience deluded—but chief over all, Satan was worshipped."[1] No doubt this was why our home and vicinity had once been the congregating place for demons, whose craving for worship was the reason for the periodical campaigns of terror designed to coerce the heathen to more fanatical worship.

[1] *Angels and Demons* (Mrs. Geo. C. Needham), p. 62.

If the heathen were convinced that their "god" had no power over us why then did they not turn in large numbers to serve our God? An answer to this question must take into account the sovereignty of God who calls whom He wills (John 6.39, 40). But the other truth is that Satan as the "god of this world hath blinded the minds of them which believe not . . ." (II Cor. 4.4). Despite many a miracle seen in Borneo, because of spiritual blindness no large numbers are coming to the Lord as a result.

CHAPTER THREE

THE BASKET GOD

"There shall not be found among you any one that . . . useth divination, or an observer of times, . . . or a consulter with familiar spirits, . . . For all that do these things are an abomination unto the Lord . . ." (Deut. 18.10–12).

I HAD OFTEN heard about the "Ouija Board", but had never witnessed its use or met with anyone else who had until recently. This occult object is manipulated by one or more people. For the purpose, they use a small board supported by castors at two points with a pencil or pen attached at a third point. At command the instrument begins to move, writing mediumistic messages on a board covered with various signs. Suggestions of trickery cannot explain everything and only a knowledge of occult powers can provide an adequate explanation.

In West Borneo the counterpart of the Ouija Board is the "Basket god". I cannot speak with first-hand experience of the Ouija Board but I can speak with some authority of its twin the "Basket god", for my wife and I have had the joy of seeing several people delivered from its snare.

Curiosity and intense desire for personal gain usually induce the unwary to consult the "Basket god".

Regular times are appointed for summoning this "god" or rather demon to answer their questions. One or more people hold a woven basket on their upturned palms, with a pen or pencil loosely tied to the basket handle. When a question is asked, the basket tips over slowly and the pen writes the answer on a sheet of paper held by another participant. Sometimes the pen and paper are put into a covered basket and the demon answers the questions by writing on the paper. If only a "yes" or "no" answer is required the basket will tip once for a "yes" and twice for a "no".

After the demon has been invited by announcing the time in the lunar month, the basket holders know that the demon has arrived when the basket becomes heavy and moves of its own accord. Many have doubted these claims until they have tested them themselves. They talk about this with great awe. The gambling motive is often involved: one young man desiring to know the winning ticket number in a lottery promised the "Basket god" his sister for a wife if he should get the winning number. Sure enough, his desire was granted and his sister became demon-possessed. For dabbling in the works of darkness there is always a price to pay.

Soon after we moved to Sungai Duri, West Borneo, we heard much talk about the "Basket god". Most of the people there had never heard the Gospel of Jesus Christ before and, not wishing to hear from our lips, many took their questions to this "god". The answers they got were a strange mixture of truth and lies, and we were horrified when we heard about it.

The demon told them that he not only hated but also feared us, although no reason was given, the object being to turn attention from the message we proclaimed to man. So we were treated rather like a powerful "god"—to be feared, but not necessarily to be heeded. Such is the subtlety of Satan!

We took the opportunity to warn the people of the danger they were in. Our neighbours were the ring-leaders, but our repeated warnings were of no avail. At night we could hear them and even see them through a crack in the wooden wall calling upon the demon. When we told them that, if they continued in these evil ways, one day the demon would come uninvited and unwanted bringing harm and mischief to the family, they only laughed at us for our trouble. Sure enough, not long after the demon struck with fury, first trying unsuccessfully to take the life of the grandmother and then successfully causing the death of a child.

During the grandmother's sickness the family called us to pray for her. This we did for she was a professing Christian of many years' standing, though the rest of the family were idolaters. After praying we again warned the family of the consequences of their evil practices. On one hand they wanted our prayers, but at the same time they were secretly calling on their idols. Then when the child fell sick they asked us for prayer, but also sought help from the spirit medium who told them quite frankly that the demon had tried to take the life of the grandmother, but had been prevented by the Christians' prayers. The demon now wanted the life of the child, and must be appeased, though, said the medium, if the child lived past a certain hour, all danger would be passed. Blood was drawn from the child's foot and used to write certain mystic symbols on coarse yellow paper. Incantations were said over the paper which was then burned, the ashes being mixed with water as medicine for the child.

When this was of no avail, the old granny urged the family to take the child to the local nurse, who sent them on to the hospital about thirty miles away. The doctor could apparently find nothing seriously wrong with the boy, who seemed well on the road to recovery. The medium's prophecy had apparently proved true, though little attention was paid to our prayers for God's glory and a victory for Christ.

When the child took a turn for the better, some of the family returned home boasting that their medium's prophecy had proved true: the child would recover. But the heathen did not have long to glory in their seeming victory; even while they were rejoicing, the child lay dead in Singkawang. The news caused them to weep with remorse as they remembered the warnings we had given. God's glory was thus vindicated and a great victory won. Several of the bereaved family trusted Christ that very day and are today some of the most active members of the local church. Praise God that demons are not omniscient; if they had known the end result of their vindictiveness, they would never have caused the death of the child. But God overruled the designs of the Evil One, souls were saved and became the foundation members of the church in Sungai Duri.

The "Basket god" was clearly seen to be feared and left alone. Ever since the events related, the villagers here lived in great fear of this "god" and will have nothing to do with him. From time to time reports reach us of others in distant places suffering similarly through this "Basket god" or demon.

We in the West should take warning. The same evil

powers that are at work in West Borneo are active all over the world. Human nature is such that if you put up a "Wet paint! Don't touch!" sign, someone is sure to touch it. After I had spoken at a Bible School in America on this subject, a few decided to see if what I had said about Ouija Boards had any truth in it. It was not long before we had a case of some very frightened and chastened young people on our hands. Being surrounded by the walls of a Christian institution and all its spiritual influences did not prevent the entry of evil spirits. All related to any branch of occultism should be left strictly alone as one would shun a red-hot poker. Idolatry and witchcraft are works of the flesh and all who call themselves "Christians" should have nothing to do with such things. "Be not deceived; God is not mocked: for whatsoever a man soweth, that shall he also reap" (Gal. 6.7).

Although divination in all its forms is hateful to the Lord, it is practised in the West under the name of spiritualism which openly admits to being necromancy or communication with the supposed spirits of the dead, which are really demons. Fortune-telling, too, can only be indulged in by the Christian at the peril of his spiritual wellbeing. Clairvoyance or insight into what is not ordinarily discernible is commonly practised in such things as astrology and some forms of hypnotism.

The "Basket god" experience certainly comes in the category of divination as an attempt to obtain covert information from the spiritual world. Its popularity in West Borneo is due to the fact that the predictions often prove accurate to a remarkable degree. Not that the spirits can predict the future, but they are often able to sway men to do their bidding in such a way that it looks as if a prediction has come true. This adds to the power they hold over the people. Holy Scripture forbids all such practices as being an abomination to God. Moses in Lev. 19.26, 31, commands, "Neither shall ye use enchantment, nor observe times. Regard not them that have familiar spirits, neither seek after wizards, to be defiled by them: I am the Lord your God." The prophets also denounce witchcraft. Isaiah writes, "And when the people . . . shall say to you, Consult for direction mediums and wizards who chirp and mutter, should not a people seek and consult their God? Should they consult the dead on behalf of the living?" (Isa. 8.19, *Amplified Bible*). Mal. 3.5 reads, "And I will come near to you to judgment; and I will be a swift witness against the sorcerers." The burning of paper on which there has been writing in blood is one form of black magic or witchcraft.

"Witchcraft," Mrs. Needham says, "was nothing short of submission to, and conscious complicity with evil spirits."[1] Paul lists witchcraft among the works of the flesh and declares that "they which do such things shall not inherit the kingdom of God" (Gal. 5.19–21). Although we live in an "enlightened age", witchcraft has by no means been abolished as some would like to believe. Germany alone has thousands of practising sorcerers dealing in black magic. I myself have talked with those who practise it, and witnessed the remarkable results of "magical" potions. Because black magic involves complicity with evil spirits, the evil spirits

[1] *Angels and Demons*, p. 88.

can cause genuine healing by the use of black magic medicine, an insidious way to perpetuate their worship. All who use such means, no matter in what form, are in rebellion against God; "For rebellion is as the sin of witchcraft (divination)" (I Sam. 15.23).

Christ is able to liberate from the bondage of black magic completely, for the promises of God's Word are true: "If the Son therefore shall make you free, ye shall be free indeed" (John 8.36). "For this purpose the Son of God was manifested, that he might destroy the works of the devil" (I John 3.8). Christ has "delivered us from the power of darkness" (Col. 1.13).

CHAPTER FOUR

STRANGE GODS

"Son of man, these men have set up their idols in their heart, and put the stumblingblock of their iniquity before their face: should I be inquired of at all by them?" (Ezek. 14.3).

DURING MY RECENT furlough I was quite amazed at seeing so many little statues of Buddha in Christian homes. True, they were there mainly for decoration, but it shocked me to discover the widespread ignorance as to the significance of these images. At one home where I stayed, my hostess had a collection of "innocent little things" as she called them. When I explained why I believed that they could become a snare to her, she was quite horrified.

"What harm can a little statue like that do? I don't worship it or use it except for a decoration." I have heard similar protestations several times.

These "innocent" little Buddhas are sold throughout the Far East as good luck charms. To rub the stomach of the statuette is said to bring prosperity. Many have little pieces of paper sealed inside them, inscribed with the very words an idolatrous priest uses to invoke the blessing of the "gods". Some have little holes where the "god" or demon can go in and out at will. The idolater treats such an object with respect, so long as it has been properly set apart for worship by the priest. Whether such objects or images used in collections or as ornaments have any sinister influence is difficult to assess. Scripture teaches that an idol has no real existence—"Well we all know that an idol is not really a god . . ." (I Cor. 8.4, *Living Letters*); cf. also Isa. 40.18–20. Figurines in wood, clay or metal are, of course, man-made, but when used as charms or idols they may become a channel for the activity of evil spirits.

But literal idol worship is not the only form of idolatry spoken of in the Bible. Covetousness, for example, is described as idolatry (Col. 3.5). We may sin against God by tolerating various unrecognized forms of idolatry in our home and life. A personal experience will illustrate my point. No one can say that the hobby of philately is idolatry, but it can easily become such. There was a time when my passion for stamps became greater than my love for the Lord. I could hardly tear myself away from the collection to prepare properly for church services. My ministry suffered and I found my heart growing cold to the things of God. I was shocked into the realization of this when a very valuable and irreplaceable collection was stolen. This proved to be the Lord's mercy to me, for only in this way did I realize that stamp collecting had become an "idol" in my life. Confession brought forgiveness and restoration.

Nor can one say that television itself is idolatry, yet it came perilously close to being so in my case. I thought I could keep myself from becoming its slave and confine my viewing to only the best programmes, but I found myself gradually watching the worthless and unhealthy programmes until my heart was again growing cold to spiritual things. This time God in His mercy allowed that T.V. set to blow out, and I realized that another "idol" had found a place in my life.

Hobbies and pleasures are not in themselves idols, but, for the Christian, *the Lord must be first* in all things. "Seek ye first the kingdom of God, and his righteousness; and all these things shall be added unto you" (Matt. 6.33).

In West Borneo where the activity of demons is so widespread, all who turn from idolatry to serve Christ know that there must be a complete break if they are to avoid trouble with demons. "No man can serve two masters: for either he will hate the one, and love the other; or else he will hold to the one, and despise the other. Ye cannot serve God and mammon" (Matt. 6.24).

In Borneo those who come out from idolatry normally invite the pastor and church members to help them destroy all idolatrous paraphernalia. The head of the home usually makes the request, and to be valid the entire family must agree. When unanimity is achieved, much prayer is offered for protection over the family. Only then do we dare to go boldly into Satan's territory and tear down the dwelling places of demons. Whatever cannot be destroyed by fire is broken into pieces and scattered far and wide.

Much faith is surely needed when these objects of Satan's worship are destroyed, for the heathen are terrified when they see it. We demand that the family involved be the first to remove the objects to be destroyed so as to assure us that they are really trusting the Lord and not following man. Their neighbours must also know that it is a voluntary act and not something they have been coerced into doing. When they have made the first move everyone joins in to help and soon all signs of idolatry are gone. Even the glue used to paste idolatrous papers on the walls and door-posts is washed off. This may sound excessive zeal, but experience has shown how necessary this is. Sometimes when just a little thing is overlooked, perhaps something a grandparent has hidden away in the attic, all sorts of trouble is apt to follow until the thing is found and destroyed. Just a little thing, as with Achan after the battle of Jericho, is sufficient to bring a curse upon the entire family.

One man in our church who turned to the Lord after being given up for dead by the heathen, had a tuberculous condition. All but the Christians were afraid of him, and he lived in poverty and filth. After the Christians had prayed for him, he was miraculously healed and seemed well on the road to full health and strength. He then asked the Christians to help him destroy his idols, but one little thing was spared, and this seemingly insignificant little thing became a stumbling block. Because of it the evil spirits refused to leave his home and soon attacked his frail body with renewed violence. Being a Christian did not protect him, nor did our prayers on his behalf. Only after the discovery and destruction of the cursed thing in his home did the "vexing unclean spirits" (Acts 5.16) leave him, and our prayers for him were answered. Today he is a wonderful trophy of God's grace and is doing the work of two men. The heathen marvel not so much at his changed physical condition, but at the moral change that has taken place in him.

Fresh from these experiences is it surprising that I felt the need to explain the significance of the

Buddhist statues to an Oriental and to warn my friends of the possible dangers involved in harbouring them? A personal experience will again illustrate the danger. A missionary on furlough spends some of his time in missionary conferences and deputation meetings. Display material and curios are in great demand and have their usefulness. It was my desire to exhibit something that would enforce my message that caused the trouble.

A few months before furlough over ten families had made a break with idolatry. Before the idols were burned, I asked permission to keep one or two objects —innocent enough in themselves: a mirror supposed to frighten demons away, hung on a door-post, a fan with mystic characters written on it, and some books containing the handwritten instructions for idolatrous worship. I kept them all in a box for use on furlough. One night my son awoke us with a terrible scream. He was having a nightmare, but no ordinary one. We found him standing on his bed as stiff as a statue with a terrified look on his face. We tried everything to calm him down, but prayer was the only relief for us and the only thing that comforted him. This went on night after night until we were almost worn out. At the time I was reading a book on demon activity and came across the statement that there is a demon behind every idol.[1] It occurred to me that the things in the curio box might be the abode of a demon and, if so, they could be the cause of our son's nightmares.

Why not? The evil unseen powers stop at nothing. If they could have brought us to a place of despair

[1] *Demon Experiences in Many Lands* (Dick Hillis), p. 23.

requiring us to leave the field of battle, their work would have been done, but praise God, this did not happen. Recognizing the nightmares as an attack of Satan, I immediately destroyed all the idolatrous curios. After confession had been made to the Lord and to the church, our son's deliverance was immediate. From that time to the present, there has been no recurrence of the nightmares and we are sobered and chastened parents.

Some have wondered whether this destruction of idolatrous property can be harmful to the people participating. We have learned from experience that whenever we destroy these things it must be in the strength of the Lord and not in the energy of the flesh. Zealous demolishing of demon shelves without meeting certain conditions is folly. When the wife of one of our most active church leaders took upon herself to destroy the idols in one of the temples, her action brought the wrath of the government down upon her head and she spent several weeks in a local jail. This was the least of her difficulties for the idolaters forced her family (with government sanction) to appease their "gods" with large contributions to the temple. This woman has ever since suffered from severe mental debility apparently brought on by oppressing spirits. One cannot rashly enter Satan's territory to destroy idols without having a prepared heart and an invitation from the interested parties to do so.

On the other hand, when people come to know Christ, we must with all boldness help them to get rid of everything connected with their heathen past. Of idolaters in Moses' day we read: "They provoked Him to jealousy with strange gods, with abominations provoked they Him to anger" (Deut. 32.16), and it is still true that without the removal of these provocations they will remain a snare. In the book of Acts there is a significant passage about the birth of the church in Ephesus which is very relevant to what we are doing in West Borneo: "Many also of those who were believers came confessing and divulging their practices. And a number of those who practised magic arts (an intricate part of demonology) brought their books together and burned them in the sight of all; . . ." (Acts 19.18, 19). That they had God's approval in this is shown in verse 20. "So the Word of the Lord grew and prevailed mightily."

Throughout Scripture idolatry is regarded with abhorrence: "Behold, ye are of nothing, and your work of nought: an abomination is he that chooseth you" (Isa. 41.24). Descriptive words such as lies, sin, shame, strange gods, wind, confusion and devils are used in describing idolatry. Neither are those who set up idols in their hearts only spared. ". . . I the Lord will answer him by myself: And I will set my face against that man, . . ." (Ezek. 14.7, 8). The Apostle John was not addressing the heathen when he penned the last words of his first epistle: "Little children, keep yourselves from idols. Amen" (I John 5.21).

CHAPTER FIVE

WEIRD PHENOMENA

"For they are the spirits of devils, working miracles . . ." (Rev. 16.14).

THERE WAS NO mistaking the excitement in the air on the day of the "moving mirror". Everybody was asking one another: "Have you seen it yet?" I gathered that it had something to do with the local temple and the large mirror hanging on the wall.

Soon Christians were asking for some explanation of this strange phenomenon. Apparently the mirror, though firmly bolted to the wall, was periodically moving backwards and forwards. Crowds were coming from all over the district to see it. My first thought was that it might be an optical illusion similar to a mirage, but this was vehemently denied. When the Christians urged me to go and see for myself, at first I refused, having no desire to walk into one of Satan's strongholds without good reason. But when they persisted, and since the heathen were demanding an explanation from the Christians, I consented to go, but only after united prayer for God's guidance and protection. We also suggested making the most of the opportunity by taking Christian literature to distribute among the crowds.

When we reached the temple the crowds were enormous. The Devil, this master deceiver of the human race, had achieved his purpose in getting the people to renew their lapsed worship by something spectacular. In West Borneo the Devil commonly uses sickness and death to fan the spark of idolatrous worship, but he uses many other devices too.

The "magic" mirror hung in a rather small temple containing all the usual paraphernalia on a table, on which were several bronze incense bowls full of burning joss sticks stuck into the ashes. The mirror was behind this shelf, and clearly visible.

A priest was standing by the table arranging the offerings brought by the many worshippers. It was apparent that he was in a trance or a state of demon possession. He was talking in an unnatural voice to another demon. There seemed to be an argument going on between the two demons, for sometimes the priest's face would contort as if in agony. At the same time he would begin to dance and as he did so the mirror moved. I watched this several times closely to detect, if possible, any trickery. The mirror, firmly bolted to the wall as it was, would move as much as a foot or so and then return to its normal position. I investigated carefully until I was satisfied that no human hands were tampering with it. It could only be the work of miracle-working demons.

The Bible speaks of such demons as "seducing spirits" working miracles in order to keep man in bondage to the evil of idol worship. I told the worshippers that this phenomenon could be of no benefit to them, but on the contrary would eventually become a snare to them all. I specifically warned the Christians to treat anything of this kind as poison, and not to be deceived by any such supernatural phenomena. On the contrary, by the Spirit of the living God, they should raise up a standard against it.

Compared to some mission fields, in Borneo we do not meet too much of this supernatural activity. But in South America poltergeist activity among heathen and Christian alike is common. Evil spirits understand the nature of people in different lands and what is calculated to bring on the greatest fear. Their aim is to receive homage from their victims through fear. "Enlightened" countries are not exempt and Satan, working as an "angel of light", works miracles there too in order to ensnare his prey.

Even Christians are sometimes plagued by poltergeist activity. A member of the Sungai Duri church, after forsaking idolatry and accepting Christ, was slow in spiritual growth and failed to live a victorious life. He was, however, a true Christian though a weak one. In disobedience to what he had been taught, this young man went to the temple to get a horoscope on his plans and so laid himself open to demon attacks. Soon, he and his wife were being terrified night after night by the sound of pots and pans flying about and other strange noises. The door was double barred, so no intruder could be responsible. Nor could rats, cats or dogs be blamed. The cause could only be demons. The couple asked for the help of the missionary and church members and, after confession and prayer, a measure of peace was given. But this man and his family have continued to have a great deal of trouble in their life.

The question arises as to how a Christian, who is protected by his position in Christ, can be troubled by demons in this way. The answer would seem to be that this young man "gave place to the devil" (Eph. 4.27) by going to the temple to seek help from a forbidden source (Acts 7.41–43). His action constituted rebellion against God and so forfeited the Divine protection. Isaiah taunted those who rebelled against God by seeking information apart from the counsel of God. "Let now the astrologers, the stargazers, the monthly prognosticators, stand up, and save thee from these things that shall come upon thee" (Isa. 47.13).

In Sungai Duri the demons use another form of engendered fear by causing mysterious fires which are beyond rational explanation. The victim will wake up in the night to see a "fire-ball" fly across the room and alight on something inflammable. When one fire is put out, another will start somewhere else. This goes on night after night until finally the individual, exhausted and in deadly fear, calls in the spirit mediums for consultation. They in turn require chickens to be sacrificed and incense to be burnt in an attempt to exorcise the demon. Thus the Devil's purpose is achieved and another worshipper is secured.

It is a profound joy to see these souls in bondage come to Christ for freedom. The Bible way of freeing the devil-possessed contrasts with local forms of exorcism. The use of the Name of Jesus is sufficient to control the demons who recognize Jesus and admit His power (Mark 5.7). It is only when these tormented people turn to Christ that they are delivered from this evil power. Nothing, positively nothing, can defeat the demons except the victorious believer who relies not on his own strength, but on the power vouchsafed to him by Almighty God and by the indwelling Christ. Time after time the demons have publicly admitted defeat. "We can do nothing, a Christian is here!" or "Our medicine cannot touch him, he is a Christian!" are common utterances. Hearing them one might expect the non-believer to come to Christ at once, but this is not so, so blinded is he by Satan.

The demons hate and fear believers. They know they are defeated but this does not stop them from continuing their activity. The heathen have no defence against their powerful and deceptive foe. No device is overlooked, and the demons never sleep: always on the lookout for a soul to enslave, they persevere until either death intervenes or their end is gained. Christ alone can make people free.

One family in the Sungai Duri church was long in bondage to these unseen powers. All but the mother of this family have surrendered to the Saviour and have been released from Satan's clutches. All but one! This tormented mother lives on in a state of perpetual fear, a fear caused by Satan himself. She recognizes the peace that the rest of the family enjoy, but seeks no relief from her fear brought on by vexing demons. Every night, promptly at eight, ghostly apparitions appear to her. Sometimes she sees bodily forms but usually only a black clutching hand. Although the mother alone can see these things, the rest of the family can feel the evil presence and the terror in the mother's eyes drives them all to pray. Prayer brings partial relief, but no permanent release for the mother. Clearly a battle is going on for this soul, the Devil and his cohorts not stopping at anything in their undying hatred for the human race. They are lost, eternally lost, but this woman's soul can be saved. Moving mirrors, fire-balls, ghostly apparitions and more must yield to the conquering Name of Jesus and the demons know it. "Thine, O Lord is the victory" (I Chron. 29.11).

"This is pure nonsense, a mere figment of the imagination," some will say. "There just are no such beings as demons!" Many books have been written on this subject, but no satisfactory explanation has been reached. The theories of the unbeliever leave much to be desired. His mind is ill prepared to grapple with that which lies outside the realm of scientific fact. Even theologians do not agree about the relationship of the supernatural and demons.

Martin Luther knew where to lay the blame, yet some would accuse him of morbidity and exaggeration.

Where do we draw the line between superstition and genuine poltergeist activity? Not all the blame can be placed on demons for the numerous superstitions held by the human race, but they certainly have their hand in most of them. We are asked to believe that the heathen are held in the grip of absurd and superstitious fears. The root meaning of "absurd" is that which is ridiculous or inconsistent with truth. After ten years of working among a civilized, yet highly idolatrous people, I affirm that the fear these people harbour of strange phenomena is not an absurd one, but is dreadfully and pathetically justified.

It is also tragic that these people, deceived as they are, should know more about demon power and activity than most Christians. On the one hand we see the cruel bondage of fear caused by these evil powers and on the other we observe ignorance and blindness brought on by these same powers who are gratified to hear their activities dismissed as "nonsense". With those who are immersed in idolatry, Satan gains his end through fear, but with those who, having the Bible, should be acquainted with the Devil's devices, his most effective work is that of deluding men into believing that all this talk of demonic activity is mere superstitious and unscientific nonsense, so fulfilling Satan's description as the one ". . . which *deceiveth the whole world* . . ." (Rev. 12.9). Clearly mere flesh and blood cannot defeat Satan. Our only hope for victory in this battle of fear and ignorance is in the Lord Jesus Christ and an acceptance of what the Bible reveals.

The Devil and his servants the demons are indeed a terrible reality, but, praise God, they have already been overthrown and rendered powerless through Christ's death on the Cross. We stand on victorious ground when we fight on the Lord's side. Did Christ not say "All power is given unto me in heaven and in earth" (Matt. 28.19)? Our Captain assured us of victory when He ascended into heaven, where He "is on the right hand of God; angels and authorities and powers" (the Devil and his henchmen) "being made subject unto him" (I Pet. 3.22).

CHAPTER SIX

POSSESSED

". . . A certain damsel possessed with a spirit of divination . . .'
(Acts 16.16).

ON THE DAY of our introduction to Red-Plum, we had a front seat view of the sad plight into which demon possession can bring a person. A little way up the street a great commotion could be heard and the air reverberated with the sound of many voices. When Red-Plum came into sight, her predicament was obvious. As she stormed up the street children and adults alike derived entertainment from making fun of this demon-tormented soul, reminding us of Prov. 12.10, "The tender mercies of the wicked are cruel." Man at times descends to the very lowest in human nature, fully revealing the corruption of man without Christ. It was clear that the woman was not just a psychopathic case, for she showed many of the evidences of being possessed. One common symptom of demon possession is the afflatus of the chest and she certainly had that. The sounds coming from her mouth did not seem to proceed from her vocal chords, but from the pit of her stomach. Moreover, our neighbours told us that Red-Plum was speaking in the Malay language, a language she neither knew nor used when in a normal state. As she passed the Christians sitting outside the Gospel Hall she was strangely quiet as if the mouth of the demon was temporarily stopped in their presence.

After passing us, however, she resumed her dancing to the cadence of filthy songs pouring from her lips. As this went on her audience bantered her and received in return all the vile contents of a reprobate mind controlled by unseen powers. Our hearts cried out to God that somehow we might be able to help her. We do not make a practice of seeking out people possessed by demons, but if they come to us we help them, provided that all the conditions are met. And so we prayed that her family would seek the help that only God can give. God answered that prayer, but it entailed a prayer battle that lasted for several months.

In the meantime some Christians who took an interest in the welfare of Red-Plum found out the origin of her possession. The details are given so as to illustrate how unclean spirits gain entrance to the human body in West Borneo. Red-Plum came from a very idolatrous family, while the father was in bondage to an avenging demon which forced him to offer "it" (a regular blood sacrifice of chickens). The failure to do so at the time appointed brought sickness and, if continued, death to the family. He had often tried to break this diabolical hold, but each time brought failure. Marriage out of the home did not free Red-Plum from this idolatrous atmosphere, but only increased her bondage by the need to worship her husband's family idols as well. Children increased her responsibilities, for when they were sick it was the custom for her or the old granny to take the proper measures: not of course to seek competent medical help even if such had been available, but to consult one of the many local sorcerers. If one failed to give satisfaction, there was always another. It was such an occasion that brought her one day to the door of an Indonesian sorceress. These sorcerers, witch-doctors, wizards, priests or whatever name they are called by, are the tools of evil spirits seeking to gain control over the unsuspecting victim. This particular sorceress was highly recommended, so why not try her? She mixed some sort of "medicine" which she, Red-Plum, was to rub on her child and on her own chest. A few days later Red-Plum became demon possessed. At once her whole personality altered. Her motherly love turned to hatred for the children and her husband. She began to frequent a temple where a notoriously immoral and wicked sorcerer lived, hoping that he would exorcise the demon or at least bring it under control. Instead, Red-Plum sank deeper into the pit of degradation that the demon had prepared for her. Because of her immoral conduct her husband had to send her back to her own home. There she wandered about the village streets cursing and being cursed by all. It was on such an occasion that we set eyes on Red-Plum for the first time.

The family almost exhausted their meagre resources seeking for a cure for their daughter. Temple after temple was visited. Sorcerer after sorcerer was consulted. Desperate and imploring efforts were made but to no avail. In the course of their quest, sixteen different priests were employed but without success. Only when their last penny had been taken by the money-mad priests were the parents ready to turn to the Christians for help.

We, of course, were praying continually that the forces of evil would be defeated. We could not go to the home until we were invited and so had to wait God's time. When at last the letter of invitation came, we gathered a band of Christians together and cycled to the parents' home. The outward evidences of idolatry in the home appalled us. We were explaining the Gospel to the family when Red-Plum entered. The friendly fashion in which she greeted us was a surprise, but this didn't last long. Excusing herself she went into her bedroom, and soon after the bedroom door flew open and out stormed Red-Plum. Her expression was so full of hate and contempt that some of the Christians were terrified. Tearing from the wall a Sunday School picture which her own brother had hung there, she stamped it to ribbons. She started to dance a sort of jig while the most filthy language imaginable flowed from her mouth. We began to pray, but in a home "protected" by idolatrous charms, we could do little for the time being. However, our prayers seemed to quiet her somewhat and she returned to her room. We took the opportunity to exhort the parents to turn to the Lord and so get rid of their bondage, explaining that we could do nothing until every last iota of idolatry was destroyed. They were taken aback at this and were not yet ready to take such a step. It was common enough for people in their community to change "gods" or to add to their number, but to get rid of all of them was unheard of! They wanted help, but were quite unwilling to risk the wrath of the spirit world by destroying their "god" paraphernalia.

At this moment Red-Plum emerged again quite violent, as if the demons had heard our conversation.

She jumped up and down on the chairs and tables chanting foul songs as she did so. When the Christians began to pray again she quieted down somewhat and my wife explained a Gospel poster to her; but we had to leave with victory apparently to the demon, because our hands were tied by the idols in the home.

The following day the Christians were informed that they needn't trouble themselves, as other means for her deliverance would be tried. The family was naturally both in fear of the demon world and of the talk of their heathen neighbours. It requires a mighty work of God for any of these people to break from idolatry and it is due entirely to His grace that so many have done so. But there were no such victories so far in Red-Plum's neighbourhood and these tortured parents had not yet come to the place where they were willing to be the first to break with idolatry. Hearing of yet other sorcerers, they tried every practice known to the heathen world. They even locked Red-Plum in her room, after beating her and binding her with ropes, but in vain. Even the priests finally gave her up as a hopeless case.

Our only recourse was to prayer. A Christian neighbour continued to visit her occasionally and even brought her one day to visit us. While in our home she seemed normal, but we were not deceived. We tried to explain the Gospel to her but her mind was darkened and she understood little. Again the invisible evil power seemed to have won a victory.

At last, when the parents reached the brink of despair, they called for us again to come. This time my wife went with a Christian teacher and got a rather shocking reception. Red-Plum tried to chase my wife out of the house with a broom, the very height of insult among Chinese. To other threats of violence my wife replied directly to the demon that she was not afraid because God would protect her. The demon was powerless to hurt my wife and could only utter words of menace. As for the parents they were still unwilling to destroy their idols, the essential condition if Red-Plum was to be freed from the demon's power. This marked another victory to the demon, but now his time was running out, as was evident by his bitter attack on Red-Plum.

We were now certain that this tormented soul could only be freed from the terrible clutches of the demon while away from her parents' home and the idols there. To this end we prayed and some of us fasted while we prayed. "Howbeit this kind goeth not out but by prayer and fasting" (Matt. 17.21). God quickly answered our prayer when once we discovered His will.

The next evening we held an evangelistic service in a house close to Red-Plum's. To our dismay, Red-Plum followed us and began to compete for the attention of the crowd standing around the door. Through Red-Plum the Devil did his wicked best to break up the service. The noise and laughter were almost more than we could stand. Tears streamed down the faces of the Christians as they witnessed this demonstration of Satan's power. I then asked the Christians to pray quietly. I knew that we had the help of Almighty God and so no one need be intimidated. As I was leading the singing Red-Plum crept up behind me and made lewd movements with her hands and body, while the heathen, obviously enjoying the proceedings, encouraged her. From Red-Plum's mouth flowed words strangely similar to the words of the "certain damsel" found in the city of Philippi who was possessed with a spirit, and made mockery of the Gospel of Jesus Christ. The enemy was clearly attempting to compromise the Gospel and to raise soothsaying to the same level as Christianity (Acts 16.16–19). Suddenly I knew without a doubt that I had to do what Paul did and command the demon in the name of Christ to come out.

I immediately told the Christians of my intention and asked them to pray that the name of Christ would be honoured that night. I then turned to the mocking throng outside and told them that they were going to see the glory of God and that Red-Plum was going to be delivered. As I spoke the words "the glory of God", something happened that I have never experienced either before that day or since to the same extent: the joy of the Lord filled my soul until I knew with Peter "joy unspeakable and full of glory" (I Pet. 1.8). The Spirit of God filled my whole being. Even the heathen fell back under this power and knew that something unusual was happening. I turned around and in the name of Christ commanded the demon to come out of her and to desist from harming her. A remarkable transformation took place before the eyes of all. A look of shocked surprise, calm and peace came over Red-Plum's face, and sinking into a chair she cried for joy over her deliverance. For the next hour I preached Christ to the silent crowd in an atmosphere of awe. The school-teachers in the audience afterwards remarked on the clarity of my Chinese and the power of the message. Personally, I was conscious only of a power greater than my own upholding me and speaking through me. God was there and His power and His glory were seen that night. ". . . the Lord spake saying, I will be sanctified in them that come nigh me, and before all the people I WILL BE GLORIFIED" (Lev. 10.3).

We soon discovered that after Red-Plum's long bout with the demon, her mind was affected. She was no longer in an evil bondage, nor did she act as she had been doing. But her failure to resume the normal activities of life and her persistent wandering made us feel that she needed medical help. We helped the family to have her committed to a hospital for mental diseases and after several months' treatment she was released. But instead of returning to her husband or her parents, she chose to go to the home of a relative in a distant village. We still see her from time to time. While her body is free from demon possession, her mind remains darkened by the "god of this world". We long to see her share the joy and peace we have in Christ. As her body was delivered from the terrible hold of the demon, her soul can also be saved from the tight bonds that hold it. Until this happens she is liable to experience the renewed attacks of the Evil One and her last state could be worse than the first (Luke 11.24–26).

Who will pray for Red-Plum?

CHAPTER SEVEN

SOLD TO A SORCERER

"Said I not unto thee, that if thou wouldest believe, thou shouldest
see the glory of God?" (John 11.40).

"IF ONLY YOU had come earlier! Honestly we didn't
think of you and now it is too late!" said Chrysanthemum's mother to her niece, Pearl.

With these words ringing in her ears, Pearl returned
home dejectedly. At the prayer meeting the same
evening she reported that her cousin Chrysanthemum
had that very day become demon possessed. Her
family had immediately consulted the master sorcerer
of the district without a thought for their Christian
relative.

Chrysanthemum had been weeding in the rice fields
when suddenly with a cry of pain she toppled over in a
dead faint. When she came to, the strange things she
said made it clear to all her family and neighbours that
demons had taken possession of her body. The news
spread quickly, and before evening large crowds had
arrived to derive what advantage they could from the
girl's supposed magic powers. The parents were
concerned, however, to have the demons exorcised,
and lost no time in calling in a master sorcerer for this
purpose. "Fu-Ya", an evil and much feared man,
soon arrived and put up his idolatrous paraphernalia
inside and outside the home. After consulting his
demons, he declared that they wanted the girl to
become a sorceress. Seeing no way out and influenced,

no doubt, by an avaricious desire for the money she could earn as a sorceress, the parents gave their consent. The superstitious heathen neighbours were excited over the prospect of having a new sorceress in the area, though they expressed some sympathy that a girl of only seventeen should be chosen.

Special clothes of red, yellow and white linen were prepared for Chrysanthemum. The procedure then to be followed was for Fu-Ya to gain control of the demons possessing the girl. To do this, he would call for his own demons to take possession of him and then in turn would attempt to control the girl's demons, so making them submissive to his will. Success would depend on whether the sorcerer's demons were higher in the demon hierarchy than the girl's. If they were not, trouble could be expected and a conflict between the demons.

Unable to indulge in the usual lechery of a demon-possessed mind in the girl's home, he arranged to have her taken to his temple, thinking that he would be more free to perform his Devil-inspired ceremonies there. But he had not reckoned on the power of God released when His saints are united in prayer.

After hearing Pearl's report we discussed what should be done. It was of the utmost importance that the parents themselves should invite the Christians to help. It would be folly to take any action without invitation. The girl had been "sold" to the sorcerer and thousands of rupiahs would be required to buy the girl back. The problems were so many that, humanly speaking, there was nothing we could do. But the resources of God are beyond human calculation and available to those who pray. And pray we did. Even as we prayed God was working, and Fu-Ya's defeat soon followed.

That very night Chrysanthemum became restless and began to demand her release. She threatened to strip the walls of his temple bare and to pull up the flowers in his garden if he refused to yield to her demands. Without knowing of my presence in the vicinity or of her cousin Pearl's interest in her affairs, she said:

"I have a cousin in Tjapkala who is helping a Great Teacher and they want me to seek the true God for help."

At this Fu-Ya became very angry and abused her freely. In the middle of the night, as the sorcerer slept, the girl silently crept out of the temple and made off on a bicycle she found handy. Then she saw what appeared to be a tall person dressed in white, who told her that she would soon be free to believe in the Lord, but that she must first return to the temple. Back at the temple she told Fu-Ya of her encounter with the "man in white" and, probably for the first time in his life, the sorcerer was really frightened. Nothing upsets these priests so quickly as a sign or omen. He quickly released the girl and sent one of his minions to remove the idolatrous objects he had put up in her home. This was to save his own face because he knew that if he didn't do this, we would.

The "apparition" was God's way to bring about the girl's release in answer to our prayers. Had she run away without the consent of the sorcerer, she would have been forced to return. God's way is perfect, no matter how strange at times.

After Chrysanthemum's return home, the family invited the Christians' help. We responded with fulness of joy, for we were seeing prayer answered in a wonderful way. We were delayed until evening, partly because the lad sent to call us played with his companions till late afternoon before delivering the message, but we accepted the delay as from the Lord. It would have been difficult in daytime to gather a team to do battle with the forces of evil, but being evening we were able to divide up, some staying behind to uphold us in prayer and the others proceeding to the scene of conflict.

Over two hundred unbelievers, hearing of our purpose, followed us to our destination. On arrival, Chrysanthemum came out to greet us and, much to my consternation and surprise, knelt down as if to give me worship. Somewhat brusquely I ordered her to stand up and to lead us into the house. It would seem that the demonic powers, knowing that they were defeated, were doing their utmost to turn attention from the true and living God to man. If the heathen watching should think of me as some kind of superior "god", their defeat would be turned into victory.

We soon discovered that Chrysanthemum's home did not belong to her parents, but was rented from her brother-in-law in return for help in his rice fields. This later gave me the clue as to why victory was turned into defeat.

Glancing around the room, I noticed that the walls were quite devoid of anything idolatrous. Chrysanthemum, however, appeared to be in a very pitiful condition. For several days she had been unable to eat and had had little sleep, as the result of the activity of these merciless "vexing spirits". I talked to her to find out how clear of mind she was. She answered my questions rationally, though a little shyly and I found no sign that she was still demon possessed. We read the Scriptures and prayed for the girl's full deliverance and protection.

We then had an excellent opportunity to preach to the non-Christians, who filled the room, with many outside unable to squeeze in. The silence was amazing under the circumstances when you consider that some were in great fear and awe of me. Others could obviously hardly restrain their desire to do me violence, so intense was their undoubted hatred for the "big-nosed foreigner" who had the audacity to interfere with their idolatrous practices. Much of their hatred was due to their frustration in being denied the use of their new found soothsayer. Their fear and awe came from the awareness that we were not vulnerable to the demon's attacks. But that strange silence provided an unforgettable opportunity to proclaim Christ and we made the most of it. Many had never heard the Gospel story before but we have reason to believe that some of the hostility to us and the Christian message was changed that night.

Chrysanthemum's family decided that it would be best for her to go and stay with Pearl for rest and care. It was well that she did so, for in the following days she was greatly in need of help. We also had the rare opportunity to observe the subtle attacks of Satan's legions of evil.

So long as she remained in Pearl's room, she seemed fairly well, though weak. Occasionally she became over-excited and indulged in unrestrained giggling. But we took this to be something physical and not as an attack from the Evil One. However, we still had much to learn.

After a few days she insisted on returning home to "get some more clothes". But she brought no clothes back with her, and we have a feeling that it was at this time, due to her physical weakness, that the demons re-entered her body.

Meanwhile Fu-Ya, already hated by many, had been completely discredited in the eyes of the heathen, owing to his inability to control the demons in Chrysanthemum. In their frustration, the heathen destroyed his equipment and forced him to leave the community. Before leaving he pronounced a curse upon all, including the Christians, and declared that the demons would return to Chrysanthemum. When we heard of this, we did not share the loss of faith in his powers, but knew that it was God's power that had prevented him from carrying out their desires. Nor did we underestimate the power of his curse.

The following day, Sunday, began bright with expectation. Several were due to be baptized and to participate in their first communion service. Little did we think that there was to be a "battle in the heavenlies" all day long.

At an early hour we learned that Chrysanthemum was moody and depressed, needing someone to be at her side continually. Sometimes she would faint. My shave in a mountain stream was hardly finished when

I was urgently summoned. The demons had again manifested themselves through the girl and some of the Christians were in great fear, and being young in the faith, did not know what to do without our help.

When I arrived, the demons cried out "We must go, we must go, the pastor is coming!" This happened several times throughout the day and seemed designed to make the people accept me as a sort of "god". The heathen who are all their life subject to these evil spirits would be deeply impressed with one to whom the demons are subject. The demons did not leave the girl in my presence, but were only in quiescence, biding their time. After earnest prayer on the part of the Christians, Chrysanthemum would awake, and how it moved our hearts to hear her beseeching prayer "Lord, save me; Lord, save me." We believed with all our hearts that God was going to answer that prayer. God gave us the promise "If thou wouldest believe, thou shouldest see the glory of God" (John 11.40). Dr. Kurt Koch, the German student of demonology, says "an often observable characteristic of the demoniac is a violent antipathy to Divine things on the one hand, and on the other a drive and longing to come to Christ".[1]

I kept near at hand and did what I could until it was time for the morning services. My wife, with a few other keen Christians, then took over the battle duties. By the time the services were over, they were almost in a state of exhaustion. The girl had needed constant attention and one or more of them were praying continually. As I approached, the spirits again

[1] *Between Christ and Satan* (Dr. Kurt Koch), p. 226.

cried out that they had to leave. It was all very embarrassing and hard to explain even to the Christians. Whenever I left and returned, the now familiar pattern was repeated.

The last time I was called was about three in the afternoon. This time I first gathered the Christians together for a time of heart-searching and prayer and we studied what the Word of God said about demon power and the conditions that had to be met before the girl could be delivered. We were powerless if any one of us harboured sin in our lives, so we confessed sin and asked God to cleanse our hearts. We also knew that we needed to banish all fear if we were to expect a victory over evil spirits and we all confessed a certain sense of fear which was perhaps the clue to our lack of power. We finally asked God to take away all doubt, and together we stood on the promise, "Greater is he that is in you, than he that is in the world" (I John 4.4). With renewed courage and strength we returned to the girl's room for the battle. We all felt that the power we had lacked previously was now present and in the name of Christ we commanded the demons to come out. They tried to choke her as they left, and artificial respiration had to be used to restore normal breathing. It was now clear to all that it was Almighty God and not feeble man who had forced the demons to leave.

What a time of praise and prayer followed! The community was deeply moved and not a few came to know the Lord after witnessing His omnipotent power. One victory had been gained, but other battles were to come. We have learned that the armour of God must be worn all the time, for the enemy only mocks when we try to do battle in our own strength. In victory, give glory to God. In defeat, seek the reason why.

"Be strong in the Lord and in the power of his might. Put on the whole armour of God, that ye may be able to stand against the wiles of the devil" (Eph. 6.10, 11).

CHAPTER EIGHT

SWEPT AND GARNISHED

"When the unclean spirit is gone out of a man, he walketh through dry places, seeking rest, and findeth none. Then he saith, I will return into my house from whence I came out, . . ." (Matt. 12.43, 44).

CHRYSANTHEMUM, LIKE ANY other teenager, is full of the love of life, moody at times and faced with the problems of growing up. Her mother had been twice married and the present husband, her father, is a ne'er-do-well drunkard. Their zealous idolatry has plunged them deep in poverty. Sickness had haunted the family for years and money that should have been spent on proper medicine has gone into the pockets of money-mad sorcerers, who live off the fat of the land.

Before leaving the village of Tjapkala we decided to take Chrysanthemum back to Sungai Duri. Three weeks remained before furlough, barely time to see Chrysanthemum back on the road to health. Weakened from her buffeting by Satanic forces, her life itself was in danger. Physical weakness makes it more difficult to resist the attacks of the Evil One, and even when victory seems secure, the demons will often return, as happened with Chrysanthemum.

It is impossible to say exactly when this took place. Perhaps it is not surprising that we were deceived into thinking that the girl was merely sick and not possessed. On our way home we had to pass the place where the girl was originally possessed; the temple where she, the Christians, and the village had been cursed by the angry, frustrated sorcerer; and the home of the parents who, unknown to us, were still consulting demon priests behind our backs. Somewhere the demon returned and for nearly three weeks we were deceived by it.

On the first day home the girl seemed well, but the next day she had fainting spells. Thinking these were due to bodily weakness, we called in medical help. No doctor was available, but a male nurse said it was a type of malaria. We believed him and he treated it as such without any success. In her fainting fits Chrysanthemum would often break out into laughter, talking and behaving queerly. The nurse assured us that this was a symptom of this type of malaria, which only added to our confusion.

All the time my wife was teaching the girl to read the Bible and to pray. Usually she was eager to learn, but sometimes she seemed to resent it and occasionally there was a strange giggling reticence. Not knowing her normal temperament we were still not suspicious, and thought that Satan was just trying to hinder her spiritual growth.

After about two weeks in our home she went out one evening with some of the other Christian girls for a walk. Suddenly she felt very tired and the girls quickly brought her back to our home. She no sooner got back than she had a very violent spell, so violent that it took several of us to hold her down. This is a definite sign of demon possession, but we were blinded to the fact and decided that she needed a doctor's care, so took her immediately to the hospital thirty miles away. On the way she began to regain her senses. As she did so, she prayed so earnestly, "Lord save me! Don't let the demons harm me!" and then prayed for all the Christians who had shown such love to her, in a way that brought tears to the eyes of those accompanying her.

She stayed in the hospital several days and seemed well on her discharge. At first she planned to spend the week-end with us as it was Friday evening, but on Saturday morning she suddenly decided to go home, and showed a stubborn determination to do so. As it turned out, we were glad that she did, for the Enemy thus revealed his hand and we knew that it was a demon and not sickness that had caused the difficulties we had had with her. By now there were only a few days left before we were to leave for furlough and we could not bear the thought of going home without knowing how Chrysanthemum was likely to go on.

On Saturday morning a few Christians, a fellow missionary and I accompanied her. At her home we left her behind while we went on to a distant village where three were to be baptized. We rode about forty miles by bicycle, preached and held the baptism service. Weary but happy we set off on our way home, only to hear the news en route that Chrysanthemum was possessed once more. Tired as I was, my first reaction was of stunned disbelief. Satan loves to get us into a corner when we are tired and practise his deceptions on our minds. Clearly something had to be done, and that soon. In our weariness we were in no condition to go into Satan's stronghold to battle with demons, and made many mistakes that night. But

71

even so, we gained more knowledge of the devices of the Devil which would help us in our future battles.

Apparently, soon after reaching home, Chrysanthemum had fallen down in a faint as the demon re-entered. Her parents had never ceased to trust in sorcerers rather than in the Lord and had been secretly going to sorcerers all the time she was in our home. This was even after witnessing the power of God in the girl's earlier deliverance at Tjapkala. They could not see that it was their own avarice and deceitfulness that were keeping her subject to demonic attacks.

Still trying to gain control of the daughter's demon, the parents took her to a sorcerer's home where many of his followers were already worshipping the spirits. As we stood watching the proceedings, our hearts cried out once again for the girl's deliverance, and so great was our concern that we disregarded our own intuitions and boldly walked into this place of evil. The priest was in a trance, but as we prayed his power was so restricted that he became very angry. Under the influence of the demons he cursed us and urged the worshippers to attack us with clubs. They clearly understood the message, but as we declared our trust in the name of the Lord and our lack of fear, they did nothing. The battle raged until nearly midnight. It was impossible for us to fight through to victory, for we were on Satan's ground. They, on the other hand, were unable to prevail because our very presence caused so much agitation among the demons. The priest repeatedly tried to control the demon in the girl, but only met with rebuff. Everyone was so frustrated that finally they consented to our making an attempt to exorcise the demon. This was one of the foolish mistakes we made that night, for with all the idolatrous paraphernalia around us the attempt was doomed from the start.

We took the girl into another room where we prayed for her and sang hymns, but nothing we did could help the girl; if anything, things got worse. Our failure brought contempt upon the name and the work of the Lord we serve. As we were singing, the demon in mockery sang along with us through the girl. This reviling of the Lord was horrible to hear and we all took turns in trying to exorcise the demon. The heathen were so disturbed that eventually they implored us to leave, saying, "The place is getting too hot for us!" We were forced to admit defeat and prepared to leave. As we did so Chrysanthemum came running through the door and implored us to take her back to our home in Sungai Duri. Knowing the importance of having the co-operation of her parents, we again asked them if they were willing to leave their idolatry, but it was like talking to the wind. Unable to take the girl with us without the parental consent, we very reluctantly left her in the hands of her tormentors.

The next day was Sunday and groups in two different villages were to be baptized. Although heavy in heart over our defeat, we refused to let Satan crowd out the victory of that occasion and went ahead with the glorious meetings in both places. When souls are being saved, the Devil is also alert, seeking ways to thwart the purposes and the work of God. That very evening in Semudun we had the joy of leading three

73

needy ones to the Lord. But our day was not to end on this note of rejoicing. We had told Chrysanthemum's parents that we planned to see them again on Sunday. Our ship was to leave early in the week, and we did not want to leave without a last attempt to help this pathetic girl.

It was late in the evening when we arrived. Everyone was up and we found Chrysanthemum wailing because of the idol altar set up in her home. When clear in her mind and temporarily free from demon control, she resisted her parents and anyone who tried to force her into idolatry. She was not deceived about the idols in her home, and knew that it was they that were keeping her in bondage to the demons. We immediately knelt around her and prayed. She seemed to be in her right mind and afterwards talked quietly with us and begged her father to let her return with us. He vehemently refused. Chrysanthemum then left the room and when she came in again she vomited. From the horrible look on her face and her reviling of Christ it was apparent that the demon had come upon her again.

In the name of Jesus we demanded that the demon reveal his name. This is Scriptural, for the name will sometimes disclose the character of the demon and thus expose his activity: "And he asked him, What is thy name? and he answered, saying, My name is Legion: for we are many" (Mark 5.9). The heathen in West Borneo know the names of all the demons in the vicinity and sometimes the demons will go to any length to conceal their identity. I don't know how many times we had to insist that the demon should give us his name. When he was finally forced to do so, it was as if an explosion had hit the room. The non-Christians were thrown into a state of panic. They were under the impression that this particular demon was far away, but here he was tormenting them again. When this demon was last in the district there was a wave of suicides among the teen-age girls. The demon's name, "The White Virgin", was appropriate enough.

When the people discovered this, they immediately called in one of their most powerful sorcerers, who talked to us for some time before warning us to move from the doorway. He proposed to summon his demon and we might be in danger. Then he began his incantations. Soon his body began to tremble and became contorted with pain as the demon took possession of him. At once the two demons tried to communicate with one another. The demon in the sorcerer, speaking in the Malay language, did not seem to understand the demon in Chrysanthemum which spoke a dialect of Chinese. The priest had therefore to call in another demon to converse with the one in Chrysanthemum. Their interchanges gave us fresh information about the character of demons. The newcomer gave his name as "Ulcerated Foot", familiar to the heathen as a demon who caused all kinds of jungle diseases, especially foot ulcers and jungle rot.

All the demons we heard speaking that night spoke as separate entities. Each voice was distinct and totally different from the normal voice of those possessed. One had a very low resonance, others were high-pitched, though not feminine. The talk sounded to my ear like the voice we hear on a long distance telephone call—clearly recognizable, but remote and distant. Spirit talk seems to be a strain, as of one learning a new language which has not been mastered. Subsequently we have heard demons use the same voice patterns as the medium would use in normal conversation, especially when the demon is pretending to have left.

As the two demons reviled the Lord we rebuked them, which only incensed them more and made them turn their wrath on us, cursing and spitting. The knowledge that they could not harm us infuriated them, for it was clear that if possible they would have torn us apart. The demon in Chrysanthemum announced that he had determined to take the girl from the time of her birth and, after waiting seventeen years for the opportunity, he was not now going to release her. He kept saying that he had no place to which to go if he was to leave her. We told him that his doom was already pronounced and that the sentence would surely be carried out. "Depart from me, ye cursed, into everlasting fire, *prepared for the devil and his angels*" (Matt. 25.41). This announcement resulted in more agitation and blasphemy. The cross of Christ was mocked and we were invited to demonstrate the death of Christ to those present by submitting to being nailed to a cross. Words cannot express the spiritual darkness we experienced in the home that night.

At one time the demons admitted the hopelessness of their condition, their voices taking on a whining note as they expressed their unwillingness to leave. Once the demon said, "If you destroy these things (indicating the idol shelf) I'll have to leave." Hearing this, the heathen threw themselves on their faces in worship with their incense sticks, and begged the demons not to leave them. With one voice they cried out that they wanted the demons and not the Lord. Later the sorcerer's demon asked the father if he wished his daughter to be a Christian or a sorceress, for if he chose the former, he would have to leave. Imagine the darkness and avarice of a heart that could reply, "Let her be a sorceress".

As never before, we realized the terrible sway Satan and his emissaries hold over these poor people. Again we left in defeat, but not before warning everyone of the consequence of their folly. We told the parents that no amount of Devil worship would bring peace to their home. Only when they were truly willing for their daughter's deliverance, and would prove it by casting out and destroying all idols, would release for the girl be possible. More than once before, prayer had turned the tide of evil and we left confident that prayer would again break the prisoner's chains and bring peace to Chrysanthemum's heart.

CHAPTER NINE

BROUGHT TO BAY

"Be sober, be vigilant; because your adversary the devil, as a roaring lion, walketh about, seeking whom he may devour" (I Pet. 5.8).

WE HAD PLAYED right into the hands of the Devil. Not only were we worsted in battle, but we were brought low in discouragement about our defeat. For days our thoughts and conversation chiefly concerned Chrysanthemum and our having to leave her before failure had been turned to victory. Nor was it encouraging on reaching home to be told that our experiences were all "fantastic dreams". But we believed that this disappointment had been permitted to teach us how to handle the weapons of warfare against these legions of evil more effectively. Samuel Rutherford once said, "The Devil is but God's master fencer in order to teach us to handle our weapons," and by God's grace we gradually emerged from our depression and were able to seek the reasons for our failure. Furlough brought rest to tired minds and bodies and we had access to good Christian libraries where we could study the subject of demonology.

We realized afresh that the failure we had experienced was not on God's part, but was rooted in human frailty. We were enabled to believe that even in the frustration caused by defeat, the purpose of God was fulfilled and that ultimately God's name would be glorified. "I am the Lord; that is my name: and my glory will I not give to another . . ." (Isa. 42.8). He showed us that one of the reasons for our defeat was our exaltation in the eyes of the heathen to be a sort of "god". As long as this was the case, we would be powerless in our personal conflict with the foe. We were also confirmed in our belief after consulting those with a similar experience, that our defeat was assured when the battlefield was on Satan's ground. The sorcerer's home was a nesting place of evil, where the idols and objects of idolatrous worship attracted the spirits and kept them in a frenzy of activity. Any attempt to do battle in these surroundings was doomed to failure from the outset.

What were we then to do? We could not forget the girl's desperate need. Her cry "Lord, save me" kept ringing in our ears. God had heard that plea, we knew, but what part had we to play in this battle? If we were not to be the instruments of God's power, who else could be?

It was essential for the heathen to realize that all Christians of whatever race or position in the Church have equal rights before God and that God is not limited in His choice of believers to do battle with the foe. The Scriptures make it plain that the work of exorcising demons is not a special gift God has imparted to select believers, but that demons must obey any victorious Christian so long as the conditions are met. Exorcism depends on our position in Christ and not a particular gift (Eph. 1.19; 2.6). We concluded that a great victory would be won for Christ if the girl were to be delivered before our return and through the medium of national Christians. Thus our only strategy was to be that defined by our Lord: ". . . this kind can come forth by nothing but by prayer . . ." (Mark 9.29).

We started a campaign to enlist everyone we possibly could in this battle to be won by prayer alone. We gave a summary of Chrysanthemum's story in our regular prayer letter, and every opportunity was taken in deputation meetings to enlist prayer warriors on her behalf. So much so that we were accused of having "only one string to our fiddle". But it got results, nevertheless.

We were impressed with God's Word to "be sober and watch unto prayer" (I Pet. 4.7). The word *sober* suggested that we were to be serious and subdued in the knowledge of the power of the foe we were fighting. We must therefore *watch* unto prayer—a watch that was to be *vigilant* or alert. We were gratified to find so many sharing this watch with us. All over the world prayers were ascending to God for Chrysanthemum. Something had to happen and daily we waited for news from West Borneo.

First reports were not encouraging. The Christians were hesitant in their follow-up, remembering the buffeting we had received and not wanting any repetition themselves. Some letters did not even mention her name and we were kept in suspense, feeling so helpless and remote from the conflict. But God in His own way and time was doing a work that was miraculous indeed.

Prayer was being answered and Chrysanthemum's family did not have a minute of peace: the drunken became more drunken, the sick more sick. Chrysanthemum herself, possessed by "The White Virgin" demon, became a moral problem. From ordinary poverty the family sank to a state of extreme poverty. But even these things failed to drive the family to seek Divine help. "The god of this world (had) blinded" their minds. They merely went from one sorcerer to another. God after god took its place on the family altar, but to no avail. They reached a state of abject misery before the break came.

Early in June 1963, an evangelistic team from Java visited the family, accompanied, rather reluctantly, by one of our fellow missionaries. He knew the danger of going without an invitation. The team sincerely hoped to do something for the girl, but there was a measure of curiosity mixed with their good intentions. Their curiosity was satisfied but they also tasted the bitterness of defeat. Nevertheless, God used their visit as a turning point in Chrysanthemum's deliverance.

While the team was in the home, the father became quarrelsome and tried to get the missionary to fight him. Refusing the outstretched hand of peace, he waved a fist of hatred. The poor man was clearly told that he alone was the obstacle between peace in the home and continued wretchedness. The only response from his warped and darkened mind was cursing. And the Christians could do nothing but retreat in disarray. How much longer was the Enemy to triumph?

Shortly after, painful carbuncles broke out on the father's body and no amount of treatment alleviated the condition. How could it? No power on earth could prevent what God was now doing. Prayer around the world was at last bringing the man to a place of willingness to part with the works of darkness. During his illness the statements and warnings he had heard from us and which had been repeated by other Christians came to his mind—namely, that "peace in his family would never come until he completely destroyed his idols and forsook all idolatry".

The news for which we had eagerly waited so long reached us shortly before sailing again for West Borneo, and our hearts leapt for joy. The father had in desperation burned all his idols, pulled up his stakes and left the community, and Chrysanthemum had at once been delivered from the demon attacks. More than one "Hallelujah Chorus" was sung in many a prayer meeting on hearing the news. But our joy was tempered with the knowledge that ours is a determined foe, and on our return to the field we found that there had been no final victory. Prayer had forced the father to acknowledge the futility of idol worship, and brought the *demon to bay*. But PRAYER—watchful and vigilant prayer—is still needed on behalf of Chrysanthemum.

We found that the father had removed all evidence of his residence in the area. Not only had he burnt his idols but his house as well. Soon the jungle was obscuring all evidences of human habitation. At first I could not trace the family about whom all sorts of conflicting reports reached us. Some said that it was not true that they had made a complete break with idolatry, but merely moved to a different community where they had adopted other "gods". Others said that they had left their idolatry and that the father was deeply ashamed of his treatment of the Christians. He admitted that since the day he cursed the missionary and Christians in general, he had known nothing but trouble.

Pressure of work prevented us from tracking down these rumours, but we knew that in answer to continued prayer God was quietly at work. At last came the opportunity I had been longing for, when I visited Tjapkala to hold a Communion service. Much to my surprise and delight, I found Chrysanthemum who had come to visit friends and to attend the service. After the service I had a long and profitable talk with her. She told me that she had been free from all demon attacks for about five months, that is, from the time her father had burnt his idols. This confirmed our conviction that idols are the natural dwelling place of demons and must be destroyed before deliverance can come. She rejoiced in her deliverance, but I sensed a certain reticence in her attitude. She seemed truly ashamed of her past behaviour. Her particular demon had ruined the reputation of many young girls in the district and had eventually driven them to suicide. Prayer had certainly saved her life, but much prayer was still needed to restore her to her place as a respectable member of the community.

Further questioning brought out the fact that her parents were still not willing to turn to the Lord for salvation. They had certainly forsaken idols, but "the god of this world" kept them blind to the Light of the world. They were still very poor and without a suitable place to live: their history was known and people were reluctant to rent property to them.

Chrysanthemum, according to Chinese custom, was no longer considered a daughter of the family, for in their difficulties she had been given to an uncle in the hope that a different name would bring relief to the girl. It was believed that the demon would be unable to find her under a different name. The uncle had given Chrysanthemum a charm which was supposed to ward off demons. The prophet Isaiah issued a stern warning against such charms "In that day the Lord will take away the finery of the anklets, . . . The pendants, the bracelets and the scarfs" (Isa. 3.18, 19, RSV). Chrysanthemum, knowing the danger of such things, had at the first opportunity deliberately lost the charm while working in the rice fields. Not knowing this, the uncle attributed her continued freedom from the demons to wearing the charm.

When Chrysanthemum invited me to the home I could see no evidence of idolatry. This proved nothing because this home was only temporary, and they would soon be moving again. At least I was cordially received and had the opportunity to bear witness and to pray for them.

I left convinced that Chrysanthemum was free from demon possession. But in her remote area she had little contact with Christians, and as her reading ability is limited, she had little chance of spiritual growth through reading the Bible. Moreover, with her parents still in spiritual darkness, she had no sympathy from them in her desire to seek Christian fellowship. The possibility of the demon returning to Chrysanthemum therefore continues. The vile "White Virgin" has departed for the present but this victory cannot yet be called final. If prayer forced the demon to leave, prayer can also bring final victory, a victorious Christian life for the girl and the conversion of her parents. Prayer is our most powerful weapon.

"Be ye therefore sober, and watch unto prayer" (I Pet. 4.7).

CHAPTER TEN

GLORIOUS DELIVERANCE

"... and from the power of Satan ..." (Acts 26.18).

A BLOOD-CURDLING scream shocked me out of my day-dreams as I sat waiting for the Sungai Duri bus. Looking up I saw six strong men trying to restrain one small, seemingly frail woman. But her strength was super-human. Even with six vice-like pairs of hands holding her, she still frequently managed to break away, attacking anyone who got in her path. People were terrified. I watched as a Chinese herbalist arrived with a tranquillizer drug. With the help of the six men, he managed to get enough of it into her mouth to relax her muscles but not her tongue. For she heaped upon us all the vile invective that only a devil-controlled mind could spew out. She too boarded the bus, and the passengers had to endure her raving for the entire two-hour journey to Sungai Duri. My only recourse was to pray for this hopeless, demon-tormented soul.

"O You who hear prayer, to You shall all flesh come" (Ps. 65.2 *Amplified Bible*).

Prayer proved the key to victory. Bunyan in *Pilgrim's Progress* tells us of Christian finding himself in the gloomy dungeon of Doubting Castle where his case seemed hopeless until he remembered the *key of promise* kept in his bosom. While he prayed deliverance came, as it always will in answer to believing prayer.

We have no mightier weapon than this against the forces of evil.

It was a full two years before the facts of Mrs. Lo's possession became known to us. They need to be told, for this case is unlike any other in our experience.

Mrs. Lo is the proud mother of seven children of whom two have been born since her days of demon-possession. Her husband is a hard-working fisherman who found it difficult to keep his family fed and clothed. Today it is easier since the children are older and able to help. But in those days Mrs. Lo's heavy burden compelled her to seek ways and means to maintain the family. Weighed down by her trials, her temper was often strained to breaking point and one day exploded. In an altercation with a neighbour, vicious abuse was hurled at one another and curses exchanged. That very night Mrs. Lo became demon possessed.

It was terrifying for the children, and the memory of it is still vivid. The evil spirit did not possess her continually, but when it came upon her she did not recognize her children, and sometimes beat them unmercifully. She would tear up everything she could lay her hands on, including her own clothes. When she asked for things that were not forthcoming, she used to chase her children with a knife and it is a miracle that no one was killed.

". . . possessed with devils, . . . exceeding fierce, . . ." (Matt. 8.28).

The nights were the most trying, for then she used to see people in the room who were long since dead, and the demon in her actually impersonated the dead

87

grandfather. When her baby cried she would answer, "How can I nurse you? I am your grandfather!"

This went on for weeks until the family were exhausted and distraught with anxiety. Sorcerers, called in to exorcize the demon, could do nothing. One of them told the family that the demon wanted the mother to become a sorceress. A master sorcerer, after a ceremony at the grandfather's grave, declared that it was his spirit which possessed her, and agreed that their only hope for peace lay in allowing her to become a sorceress.

Considering the awe in which the heathen hold their priests, the husband's stern refusal to allow his wife to become a sorceress is amazing. He tried other means to bring about her release, including competent medical treatment, but this also was unavailing. Without the recognition of demonic influences at work, the doctor was little better off than the quack doctors with their charlantanism. During her stay in the hospital, nurses had difficulty in keeping clothes on her and at times several strong men could not control her. "For ofttimes it (unclean spirit) had caught him: and he was kept bound with chains and in fetters; and he brake the bands, . . ." (Luke 8.29). When the demon left her for a period she was at a loss to know why she was in hospital. Nor did she know how she had been behaving while possessed, or sick, as she called it.

Since the doctors were unable to do anything, the husband took her home again, and it was then that I saw her for the first time at the bus station.

Soon after Mrs. Lo's return home she expressed a

deep longing to come and see us, although she had never met us and without knowing why—a longing doubtless prompted by the Holy Spirit in answer to prayer. Even when "ill" she would try to come, saying that she had the same surname as ours. At first the family restrained her, but finally gave way, as hearts were softened toward us through our testimony to a dying relative.

One day her sister came from the city to see her and brought her to us. The Christian neighbour who had also encouraged her introduced her to us. I was away at the time, but my wife welcomed the little group and listened to the story.

Knowing nothing of the woman's past, and unaware that the neighbours were really frightened of her, my wife could see that she was greatly in need of help. Even then she was fairly sure that the difficulty was Satanic. After listening attentively for the very first time to the Gospel explained to her with the help of pictures, she said,

"It's true, I know it's true, my heart tells me it's true."

Her heart was one truly prepared by the Holy Spirit to receive the Word of God. She accepted the Lord as her Saviour on that very first hearing and for several weeks continued to come each day for teaching and prayer. If we were away one of the Christians would play Gospel recordings to her. She had been completely freed from all attacks of the Evil One and continued to praise God and to witness to what God had done for her.

I had previously been of the opinion that no one

could be delivered from demon possession until the demon was commanded to depart. But from this experience we have concluded that possessed persons can sometimes be delivered by prayer alone. Had Mrs. Lo been permitted to become a priestess there would have been more grounds for the demon to indwell her permanently, making her the tool of a "familiar spirit". Persevering prayer, fasting, and certainly the word of authority would then have been needed to drive the evil power out of her. As it was, the demon had not gained full control, possibly because of her husband's stand, and her own unwillingness. It is also significant that Mrs. Lo became a child of God when away from the home, and when she was not under direct attack from the demon.

Satan and his minions hate both prayer and the Word of God. When prayer was made the Holy Spirit moved Mrs. Lo to come to Christ for her deliverance. Then the demon had to leave. "How fearful are the powers that stand behind all the sin and misery of fallen mankind. But how powerful and just is God! He conquers the foe, makes manifest His own victorious power; and to those who take their stand on His side He gives eternal life."[1]

Shortly after Mrs. Lo's deliverance from the powers of evil, she bought a Bible. Nor did she let the dust collect on it, but read it constantly and even slept with it close beside her, finding comfort in its message. Her joy in the Lord and willingness to witness remain to this day. Give glory to God.

"Lord, teach us to pray, . . ." (Luke 11.1).

[1] *From Eternity to Eternity* (Erich Sauer), p. 88.

CHAPTER ELEVEN

THE GREAT DECEIVER

". . . called the Devil, and Satan, which deceiveth the whole world . . ." (Rev. 12.9).

DECEIVED! The very sound of the word causes disgust and resentment. No one wants to admit to having been deceived, but that is what the Bible says is true of some Christians. "Now the Spirit speaketh expressly, that in the latter times some shall depart from the faith, giving heed to seducing spirits . . ." (I Tim. 4.1). Clearly some genuine Christians are deceived, for one cannot "depart" from the faith without first belonging to it. Repulsive as it is, there are those who have been cunningly and maliciously beguiled. As Eve was beguiled by the Serpent, so the child of God can be misled by this arch-deceiver's strategy.

Scripture tells us that as the time approaches for the final overthrow of Satan and his hordes of evil, his wrath will increase and his deceptions multiply. "Woe to the inhabiters of the earth and of the sea! for the devil is come down unto you, having great wrath, because he knoweth that he hath but a short time" (Rev. 12.12).

We are living in momentous days when the on-slaughts of deceiving spirits seem to have reached a fearful crescendo—a fact of which the Church cannot afford to be ignorant. How can Christians allow their fellow believers to suffer from Satanic attacks through ignorance of Satan's devices? Everything possible must be done to understand and to expose these deceptions. Dr. Unger writes: "Many shrink from the subject altogether, insisting that so long as Christ is preached, occupation with Satan and demons is unnecessary and spiritually unhealthy."[1] While there is danger in an excessive and unhealthy interest in demonology, there is an even greater danger of allowing Satan to win the battle by default. When we refuse to assimilate the knowledge needed to expose his tactics, Satan gains an advantage over us as the Apostle Paul well knew. "Lest Satan should get an advantage of us: for we are not ignorant of his devices" (II Cor. 2.11).

It is clear that Satan is working mischief in the churches: what church has not seen some of its most promising converts become victims of demonic delusion and influence? What church has not been shaken to its very foundation by schisms and conflicts between church members as a result of Satanic deception? What church does not have members who are "tossed to and fro, and carried about with every wind of doctrine" (Eph. 4.14) at the bidding of deceiving spirits? A reading of Scripture reveals that the armies of the invisible world are doing their utmost to hinder the witness of the Church of Jesus Christ. The secret of how they do so is all found in the word DECEPTION.

Deception takes varied forms: there is the deception of the unregenerate; of the weak Christian; and of the spiritual believer. In each case Satan has a special approach, but the end result is the same—the soul deceived and Satan's purpose accomplished.

[1] *Biblical Demonology*, pp. 201-202.

It is not hard to understand how the unregenerate can be deceived. As "sons of disobedience" their pathway of life follows the course of this world, where the control is in the hands of the "prince of the power of the air" (Eph. 2.2), a fact which is often unrecognized. When man denies Christ, like it or not, he comes under the dominion and direction of Satan, which leaves him wide open to every form of deception Satan may use in order to keep him in bondage to the old sinful nature. This is true of the atheist, the agnostic, the sceptic or the indifferent.

In our missionary work careful attention must be given to idolatry as a device of Satan to deceive man. By it Satan achieves his aim of keeping man in disobedience and rebellion against God. Idolatry is a delusion which beguiles man into thinking that his way is right. "There is a way which seemeth right unto a man, but the end thereof are the ways of death" (Prov. 14.12). The idolater may admit that his religion is one of fear, but he will not admit that it is wrong, sure proof that he is the victim of deceiving spirits. How else can one account for this nonsensical system which the Psalmist derisively describes: "Their idols . . . are the work of men's hands. They have mouths, but they speak not: eyes have they, but they see not: . . ." (Ps. 115.4–8)?

In West Borneo people do incredible things in the name of idol worship. It is common to see idol worshippers offering their sacrifices of food by the roadside, to appease the spirits. The local fisherman will not dare to go out to sea until he has worshipped his own special "god". The dead may not be buried until every detail of the idolatrous ceremony has been carried out; even driving the nail in the coffin demands a special ceremony of its own, to ignore which would allow the spirit of the deceased to come back and haunt them. The sick are specially active in idolatry, often handing over their soul to the temple priest for safe keeping! They do this by placing their nail clippings in a small urn, which is then wrapped in a cloth of white, blue and red, these colours together supposedly having the power to keep the soul of the sick locked up in the urn. The idea is to prevent the disease from spreading.

Foolishness? How can anyone be so blind as to believe in this sort of thing? It is not foolishness to these benighted people, who worship the idols in all seriousness, being victims of Satan's deception.

Idolatry may not be suited for deceiving the so-called "enlightened" people who regard it as humbug and superstition, a hang-over from dark ages. But Satan's deception becomes more subtle as he deals with the educated, religious heathen. This type may be strongly religious, but at the same time utterly Godless: "Having a form of godliness, but denying the power thereof" (II Tim. 3.2–5). As one for whom we had much hope at one time remarked, "It is all right to be a Christian, but don't let it be your master."

Deception concerns not only the unregenerate, but also the weak and carnal Christian, those who have been able to escape from Satan's clutches. His purpose now is to keep the new Christian from becoming useful and fruitful, and his wiles are many. For example:

The Christian is deceived who thinks he can do whatever he wishes and yet not be punished (Gal. 6.7).

The Christian is deceived if he thinks he does not need to put into practice that which he learns of Christian truth (James 1.22).

The Christian is deceived if he thinks he is a righteous person and without sin (I John 1.8).

The Christian is deceived if he thinks bad company will not ruin his morals (I Cor. 15.33).

If these are not enough to enslave the carnal believer, Satan has other devices to deceive, such as the many false teachers that will arise. "And many false prophets shall rise, and shall deceive many" (Matt. 24.11).

In our work we have several instances of those who, because of their weakness, have been totally deceived. Snow Plum is a tragic example. She was one of the first to attend the Gospel services held in Sungai Duri. She was also among the first to make a decision to follow Christ. Her early testimony was victorious and it was a joy to hear her pray. As the day approached for her baptism, the Devil struck with all his fury. She had permission from her parents to be baptized and apparently no obstacle remained. Deception first came to Snow Plum through the maternal grandmother whom Satan has long used in this community to spread his lies. She told the parents that the girl ought not to be baptized, for "fear of the future"—a reference to marriage prospects especially. She probably feared too that there would be one less to worship her spirit when she died. As, in this community, a grandmother's word is greatly respected, permission for her baptism was withdrawn at the last minute. Snow Plum was crestfallen and the stage was set for Satan's masterpiece of deceit. Snow Plum had believed that permission to be baptized was an answer to prayer, but when this was withdrawn the Devil whispered in her ear, "Does God really answer prayer?" Thereafter one deception followed another. She was deceived about evil companions, about worldly amusements, and finally and worst of all, that if she ceased going to church, persecution from her family and friends would end. Every conceivable form of deception was used and the "fiery darts" (Eph. 6.16) accomplished their purpose.

Some might say that the girl was never saved in the first place, but that is too easy an explanation. We know the girl and can testify of the witness she bore before these events. It would seem that this girl, like some of the Corinthian believers, was permitted to become a captive of Satan. "To deliver such an one unto Satan for the destruction of the flesh, that the spirit may be saved in the day of the Lord Jesus" (I Cor. 5.5.). This was also the experience of the two believers mentioned in I Tim. 1.20 who were deceived into propagating false doctrine. Mrs. Needham says, "No words of the Epistles are more mysterious and awful than these. It is the case of a child of God, once made free through the truth, and for some time walking in the life and light of the Gospel, having lapsed, he is, by the edict of his heavenly Father, delivered back to the bondage of Satan, for the possible recovery of the spirit from eternal condemnation."[1]

Mien-Kuang was a boy with a bad reputation before he experienced the regenerating power of God. No one

[1] *Angels and Demons*, pp. 106–107.

welcomed his companionship. After his conversion there was an amazing change and his teachers bore witness to the transformation. Instead of being among the most stupid and dull in the class, he became intelligent and among the bright boys at the top of the class. His zeal in attending all the church meetings and in participating in the church activities was a remarkable testimony. Yet, when he fell a victim of Satan's deception, the "thud" was heard throughout the land.

The clue to Mien-Kuang's fall is probably found in I Tim. 3.6—"Not a novice, lest being lifted up with pride he fall into the condemnation of the devil." Pride was his downfall, for through it the Devil found an entrance. "Pride goeth before destruction, and an haughty spirit before a fall" (Prov. 16.18). It was natural to be happy about his school successes, but when he began to brag about them and not to give God the glory his downfall was certain. "God resisteth the proud" (I Pet. 5.5). After that the downward steps in his deception were rapid. The "father of lies" (John 8.44) made him a master of lies. The Deceiver made the deceived a master of evil deceit. Today Mien-Kuang remains morally helpless in the grip of evil.

From these two instances it can be seen how the method of deception is varied to suit the special circumstances of the victim. But whatever plan is used, Satan and his emissaries persevere until the end is achieved and the deceived are ensnared. Defeat for the Satanic powers comes only when the believer recognizes the peril and is on guard against it. In peaceful times we tend to let down our defences to our confusion and shame; then at the first sign of danger, we hasten to build up our defences, often too late. Scripture provides ample warning of the peril of deceiving spirits and the means of defence against them. Let us not lose the battle through ignorance of Satan's devices or by thinking "it could never happen to me!".

But it is with the spiritual believer that the keenest battle is fought. The scene shifts from deception of the things of the world and the flesh to things spiritual and a battle in "the heavenlies". The Apostle Paul describes the warfare of the spirit-filled believer against the powers of darkness: "For we wrestle not against flesh and blood, but against principalities, against powers, against the rulers of darkness of this world, against spiritual wickedness in high places" (Eph. 6.12).

We may ask "How is Satan able to deceive us in things spiritual?" The answer in part is found in our Lord's words in St. Matthew's Gospel, "Take heed that no man deceive you. For many shall come in my name, saying, I am Christ; and shall deceive many. For there shall arise false Christs, and false prophets, and shall shew great signs and wonders; insomuch that, if it were possible, they shall deceive the very elect" (Matt. 24.4, 5, 11, 24). It appears that the full force of deceiving spirits is directed against the spiritual believer in doctrinal rather than in worldly matters, although the latter may be used after the believer has been ensnared by the more subtle means. In I Tim. 4.1–2, the Apostle Paul gives a full account of how wicked spirits attack the spiritual believer and by deception beguile him away from the faith through the use of false prophets.

Matt. 24.24 "and shall shew signs and wonders" suggests that the clue to this kind of deception is in "signs and wonders". Today the true is being counterfeited on every hand by the false. The false prophet through Satan's power is able to perform genuine miracles in the name of Christ, and so to ensnare the saint of God. He is made captive because he accepts everything supernatural as necessarily Divine, forgetting that Satan can and does counterfeit the activity of God. "And I saw three unclean spirits like frogs come out . . . of the mouth of the false prophet. For they are the spirits of devils, working miracles . . ." (Rev. 16.13, 14). See also II Thess. 2.9 and Rev. 13.13, 14. In the last days we can expect a great multiplication of demonic manifestations and that many devout and sincere Christians will be deceived by these manifestations, so making shipwreck of their faith.

In my early days our family belonged to a branch of the Christian Church that placed great store by the supernatural. We had a deep and sincere longing for a closer walk with God, but were deceived by lying spirits into believing that this closer walk could be obtained through what we now see to be a false interpretation of the Word of God. Suffice it to say, the Christian must avoid being swayed by the apparent miracles in the so-called "healing movements" or in the modern "tongues movement". "Believe not every spirit, but try the spirits whether they are of God: because many false prophets are gone out into the world" (I John 4.1). God definitely warns us not to believe every spirit, but to test or try the spirits according to I John 4.3. If this command is ignored, we throw ourselves open to Satanic deception. I am thankful for the healing balm of the "Great Physician", and for the gifts God bestows on His children, but let us be constantly on the alert against the evil malicious Deceiver who, in the higher range of the spiritual life, counterfeits the workings of God through a dazzling array of "signs and wonders".

"Mankind tumbles today from one sensational news to another. A scintillating line of miracle workers, healers, saviours and helpers dance before our eyes. Who can still see clearly?"[1] Thank God, He has made a complete provision for the recognition, exposure, protection, and immunity from the assaults of these crafty agents of evil.

"Finally, my brethren, be strong in the Lord, and in the power of His might. Put on the whole armour of God, that ye may be able to stand against the wiles of the devil" (Eph. 6.10, 11).

[1] *Between Christ and Satan* (Dr. Kurt E. Koch), p. 192.

CHAPTER TWELVE

WITCH-DOCTOR

"They hatch cockatrice' (marg. adders') eggs and weave the spider's web: he that eateth of their eggs dieth, and that which is crushed breaketh out into a viper" (Isa. 59.5).

ADDERS' EGGS, the poisonous offspring of the serpent, and yet so innocent in appearance that many are deceived to their own destruction! Such is the witch-doctor, truly a viper's brood who will sting to death all who fall into their hands. From time immemorial these human leeches have represented and perpetrated evil. It is so in West Borneo.

On the one hand there is the evil power of the Devil, and on the other the inborn evil of man's heart, ever willing to become Satan's tool. The witch-doctor or sorcerer represents man whose heart "is deceitful above all things and desperately wicked" (Jer. 17.9), while Satan is the one who ever since creation has attempted to seduce and to destroy the human race.

Scripture tells us that the Devil subverted man by casting doubt on the veracity of God's Word. "Hath God said?" queried the subtle Tempter. By the time of the flood Satan had subverted the human race so completely that God had to say "I will destroy man whom I have created from the face of the earth" (Gen. 6.7). Man had had ample warning of Satan's devices, but his innate desire to penetrate into mysteries over which the Almighty has drawn a veil, ". . . intruding into those things which he hath not seen . . ." (Col. 2.18), provided Satan with the device of sorcery to infiltrate human society and to subvert it. The Pentateuch contains many references to the practice of sorcery among heathen nations. This practice was prohibited and there is reason to believe that God ordered the destruction of many of these people because of their being utterly given over to it in their worship. Hebrew law contained the death penalty for a medium (Ex. 22.18; Lev. 20.27) and also a stern warning that such as "turned after them" would be cut off from among their people (Lev. 20.6). It is a sad commentary that after repeated warnings and Divine judgments, man persisted in the diabolically evil art of witchcraft. Even Saul, the first king of Israel, when he sought counsel from a necromancer did not escape God's wrath; "Saul died for his transgression which he committed against the Lord, even against the word of the Lord, which he kept not, and for asking counsel of one that had a familiar spirit . . ." (I Chron. 10.13–14). Later on, the Hebrew nation as a whole fell under the corrupting influences of idolatry and paid for their iniquity by being dispersed among the nations surrounding them.

The Old Testament describes a sorcerer in Deut. 18.10, 11 as one who—

"useth divination" or is an expert in divining by the aid of magic.

is *"an observer of times"* or one who practises hidden arts.

is *"an enchanter"* or diviner by serpents.

is *"a witch"* or a mutterer.

is "*a charmer*" or a joiner of words together for incantation.

is "*a consulter with familiar spirits*" or an enquirer of the indwelling demon.

is "*a wizard*" or a false prophet.

is "*a necromancer*" or a seeker unto the dead.

All these terms are more or less interchangeable and belong to the same function of sorcerer. The New Testament, summing them up in the one word "sorcery" (Acts 8.9), also condemns the practice. We find this is Paul's indictment of Elymas the sorcerer. ". . . O full of all subtlety and all mischief, thou child of the devil, thou enemy of all righteousness, wilt thou not cease to pervert the right ways of the Lord? and now, behold the hand of the Lord is upon thee, . . ." (Acts 13.10, 11).

We live in times when sorcery and black magic are either laughed off as superstitious humbug or looked upon as diversions to entertain. Some Christians ignore them altogether as relics of the "dark ages". And yet, today, many German villages have people called witches who profess direct communication with the spirit world. It would shock many to know that belief in sorcery is the living, working creed of over half the human race. The "spider's web" of the sorcerer is still being spun over most of the world and nowhere is it more prevalent than in West Borneo. Over the past ten years we have seen every type of vileness perpetrated by the sorcerer. Through subtlety and craft, they have successfully lorded it over the masses, and only in recent years have their cunningly wrought webs been torn apart by the saving Gospel of Jesus Christ.

According to Deut. 18.10, 11 the sorcerer is one that *uses divination*: that is, he claims to be expert in the art of predicting future events by the use of magic and secret ceremonies. To do this the sorcerer must be completely in league with the Devil. He starts his divination by invoking his "familiar spirit", in a similar way to the Christian's prayer to God, except that the sorcerer uses the known name of the spirit. Then magic charms are brought into play. In our area the most common are blocks of wood not unlike large dice, which, when tossed on the ground after the preliminary invocation, fall in such a way as to give the answer to the sorcerer's question. I personally can testify to the sorcerers' diabolical ability to predict future events, not by their own intelligence, but as the result of their alliance with the works of darkness. These sinister forces can so influence a man that the sorcerer's prediction is realized in the course of events.

Where does this deadly device of Satan to entrap the unwary leave the one who follows it? Magic help must be paid for dearly. The witch doctor, while he may give apparent help for a time, can only tear down and destroy. For instance, lottery is big business in West Borneo and a large portion of the population is involved in it in some way. Much of the sorcerer's time is taken up in predicting winning numbers. We have often listened to the boasts of those who have won large prizes through the use of magic, but later inquiry has revealed broken lives, broken homes, insanity and even suicide as the ultimate fate of the successful prize winners. "Be not deceived; God is not mocked: for whatsoever a man soweth, that shall he also reap" (Gal. 6.7). All use of divination is like the "spider's web" and, as the Bible predicts, "Their webs shall not become garments, neither shall they cover themselves with their works: their works are works of iniquity, . . ." (Isa. 59.6).

A sorcerer is, in the second place, a *consulter with familiar spirits*. The Word of God warns us to "turn not unto them that have familiar spirits, nor unto the wizards; seek them not out, to be defiled by them: I am Jehovah your God" (Lev. 19.31). The "familiar spirit" is the divining demon present in the body of the sorcerer. This spirit is on intimate terms with its host and can be summoned at will by him. It can also be dismissed when its work is done. We have watched these priests call up their spirits and it was a hair-raising experience. After the ceremony of worshipping the demon by way of preparation, followed by the invitation to come, the body of the sorcerer goes through violent contortions as the demon enters. When possession is complete, the demon speaks through the vocal chords of the demon possessed sorcerer to an assistant, while it is the assistant's responsibility to interpret the demon's counsel. It is important to note that when the believer is in Satan's territory, the work of the sorcerer is largely unhindered. Prayer seriously frustrates his activity only when the sorcerer is out of his sphere of influence.

Not everyone who is possessed with an evil spirit has a familiar spirit. It is only when the possessed person consents to become an agent of the demon that the spirit becomes "familiar". In other words, there is an intimate family-like relationship between the demon and the agent who consents to do the will of the evil spirit. I have asked several sorcerers who were willing to talk to me about the circumstances of their becoming witch doctors. In every case it started with illness. In seeking healing through the use of magic as prescribed by a sorcerer they opened the way for a demon to possess them. Not everyone who uses magic when ill becomes demon possessed, however. Some develop serious psychic disturbances and become obsessed if not possessed. To account for possession in some cases one has to realize that demons are dis-embodied spirits, who are always seeking a body congenial for their use (Matt. 12.43, 44). Before a demon can gain entrance into the human body, certain conditions must be fulfilled. When an indivi-dual is sick his resistance to demonic attack is low, but when he is both sick and a consulter of witch doctors, he leaves himself completely open to attack and pos-session. When there is also consent to become an agent of the demon, then the possessed becomes a sorcerer and the familiar spirit has found a home.

The degree of the witch doctor's effectiveness as a sorcerer depends on the position or authority his familiar spirit has in the realm of evil spirits. Dr. Unger says, "The serried spirits can be none other than his angels or demons with different stations of rank and responsibility, who are the unseen though real agents behind the visible human actors in the great world drama enacted in this wicked world system."[1]

[1] *Biblical Demonology*, p. 53.

Although Divine revelation is silent regarding the degrees of authority in Satan's realm, there can be very little doubt that the demons do have a highly organized empire of evil. I myself have heard through the lips of possessed persons, two demons arguing over disputed territory. It seems that the demons are given boundaries over which they are not allowed to pass. Again I have heard demons trying to assert authority over other demons. If the one trying to usurp authority is lower in rank than the other one, there is apt to be violence. On the other hand, if the demon is high in rank, other demons must submit to his higher authority. For this reason too, there are different ranks of sorcerers. In a heathen community they are graded according to their efficacy as mediums. Thus you have the master sorcerer and those with various ranks below him.

The sorcerer is also expected to be expert in a wide range of Satan's arts. By communication with familiar spirits they are supposed to possess extrasensory knowledge and thus are called "*wizards*" in Deuteronomy 18. Sometimes this supernatural knowledge is revealed by means of the medium, as when the ill enquire about their sickness and its cure; or when the betrothed enquire about the best day to be married; or when the gambler seeks a lucky number for his lottery ticket; or the builder a suitable construction date; or a bereaved family the proper day and hour for burial, etc. The whole heathen community is thus given over to seeking out covert information from the spirit world and so becomes its slave. Satan has accomplished his purpose; the adder's egg has been devoured, the swallower poisoned and the unwary has been ensnared in the Devil's web.

A third title of the sorcerer is *"the witch"* of Deuteronomy 18 where the word is translated "sorcerer" in the Revised Version. The Hebrew word denotes one who practises magic by using occult formulas, incantations, and mystic mutterings, far removed from the childish conception of an old woman riding on a broom stick, poisoning people by the use of some magic formula. The word "charmer", also found in the book of Deuteronomy, is to all practical purposes the same as "witch".

Elsewhere in this book is the case of a sorcerer using the patient's own blood to make magic medicine for him. Fetishes such as finger nails and hair sealed in an urn are also used either to contain the disease or keep it from spreading to others. Such urns are also used to "contain" the spirit of the sick one. This is often done in the case of an ailing child, and the covered urn hung in the rafters to keep the child's spirit from leaving the home. Incantations and mystic mutterings by the sorcerer are heard during a funeral. Each stage from death to burial has its own special ceremony in which incantations are chanted. Years after death the surviving members of the family still call the priests annually to repeat these incantations, believing this to be necessary for protection from the dead person's malicious spirit or ghost.

The final title of the sorcerer is *"necromancer"*, the literal meaning of which is "one who seeks unto the dead". He is one who seeks information from the spirits of deceased persons. I do not believe that anyone, spirit medium or otherwise, can communicate with the dead, for Scripture teaches that the dead have no portion with the living (Eccles. 9.5, 6). The heathen and indeed our western "spiritualists" who attempt such communication are deluded by the master liar. Dr. Unger says, "Facts are not lacking to indicate that modern spiritualism is nothing more nor less than ancient sorcery revived, with particular emphasis on communication with the supposed spirits of the dead, which are really deceiving, impersonating, demons, so that the phenomenon is basically demonism."[1] From my personal observation, seducing demons are able to imitate the voice of the dead and to ensnare their victims by accurate disclosures of the dead person's history or of facts that only relatives could know. It can be seen what a diabolical web Satan and his emissaries are spinning to trap the unwary. Dr. Irvine tells us, "What messages are received from the spirit-world are not received from those who have passed through the veil, but from demons who impersonate them."[2]

God's indictment of necromancy is equally clear. "And when the people shall say to you, Consult for direction mediums and wizards who chirp and mutter, should not a people seek and consult their God? Should they consult the dead on behalf of the living?" (Isa. 8.19, *Amplified Bible*).

Among the heathen Satan does not need to veil his operations; he has no need for stratagems and disguises. His sway is easy and unhindered except where

[1] *Biblical Demonology*, p. 158.
[2] *Heresies Exposed* (William C. Irvine), 11th ed., p. 175.

Christianity has exposed his "lying wonders". How thrilling it is to see the soul once bound in Satan's grip released by the mighty hand of God! But my ear still rings with the piteous cry of one sorcerer who wanted to be released from his bond to the devil. This young lad, hardly out of his teens, became possessed and, as the community wanted to increase the ranks of local priests, he had no choice but to become a medium at the will of his familiar spirit. Because he was possessed by a high ranking demon, the demands on his mediumship were tremendous and life for him was very hard. Once when he fled to a distant city he found a measure of freedom, but was soon forced by the village elders to return under penalty of death if he refused. When I told him that the Son of God could make him free, he looked at me with tears and said, "Pastor, what you say is true, but if my people even know that I have been talking to you, they would want to kill me." Another sorcerer told my wife that "The way of the sorcerer is very bitter, but what can be done about it?" The stark hopelessness of their condition without Christ presents a continual challenge to the Christian Church in West Borneo.

Praise God, we in West Borneo can witness to the fact that five former sorcerers have had their fetters broken by the Almighty hand of the great Victor ot Calvary. The power of Christ has snatched them from Satan's dominion and has set them completely free. Four live in areas outside our district, but they have a good testimony and are active in their local church. The fifth I only recently led to Christ. It was from this man, Mr. Chien, that I learned many of the methods

Satan uses through sorcery to ensnare his victims and to keep them in bondage. It is too early yet to say that Mr. Chien is living a continuously victorious life, but he is showing much promise. As a Christian and through his vital union with Christ, he is in a place of complete security from the forces of evil that once controlled him. As a child of God, he will continue to be the target of the "fiery darts of the wicked one" and the conflict is real. Satan is not happy that his former slave has been released from the fearful web of death. But thanks be to God the "adder's eggs" have been spurned and the "spider's web" has been cast aside.

"If the Son therefore shall make you free, ye shall be free indeed" (John 8.36).

CHAPTER THIRTEEN

THE QUERY

"Happy—(blessed, fortunate and enviable)—is the man who finds skilful and godly wisdom, and the man who gets understanding—drawing it forth from God's Word and life's experiences" (Prov. 3.13 *Amplified Bible*).

"THERE ARE TWO equal and opposite errors into which our race can fall about the devils. One is to disbelieve in their existence, the other is to believe and to feel an excessive and unhealthy interest in them."[1]

It is not hard to understand when the non-believer falls victim to the designs of Satan and refuses to believe in his existence and activity, for his mind has been blinded by the "god of this world" (II Cor. 4.4). But what is hard to understand is the complete indifference, the surprising ignorance and, in some cases, the actual hostility in some Christian circles in relation to the truth about demonology. On a recent furlough I found a genuine hunger among Christians to understand what is behind the present unrest and conflict in the world. In the main this desire is not being satisfied for three reasons: a disbelief in the existence of a hierarchy of evil powers at work influencing the passions of man; the fear of an excessive and unhealthy interest in the subject; and a lack of knowledge about demonology.

As to the first, the opinions of man have never changed the facts revealed in the Bible, and learned by

[1] *The Screwtape Letters* (C. S. Lewis), Preface.

bitter experience. The Bible declares that Satan exists and possesses great power and influence over the activities of man, while experience has shown that this is irrevocably true.

The dangers in an excessive preoccupation with demonology are often exaggerated. Man's conquest of many preventable diseases is the consequence of a highly organized campaign of public information. You fight fire with fire, and half-hearted teaching of demonology for fear of stirring up an unhealthy interest will only feed the fire. The Christian is able to defeat the foe because he is ". . . not ignorant of his devices" (II Cor. 2.11).

The matter of ignorance can only be solved by the individual himself. Much has been written on the subject, but it has not always been authenticated by field experience. The Bible, however, contains a rich store of information on demonology, available to all who will look for it. Most Bible book stores carry a number of good books on this subject and they would be glad to help anyone in the selection of pertinent research material. May God give the strength, courage and perseverance to anyone who wishes to pursue this study. The rewards are immense.

The present chapter was written after receiving suggestions from fellow missionaries who had read the unfinished manuscript. No doubt the reading of *Roaring Lion* will provoke many questions and it is my sincere desire that this chapter will answer some of them.

I. *What is the origin of demons?*

Down through the ages, amid much speculation

some absurd theories have been advanced regarding the origin of demons. This has been partly due to the definite reserve of Scripture concerning their genesis, a silence which surely suggests that the important thing is not where the demons came from, but that they do actually exist, and that a ceaseless warfare must be waged against them. Nevertheless the question is legitimate and one that is often asked.

Dr. Bancroft says, "Demons are an order of spirit beings apparently distinct and separate from angels, and which from the intimations of certain passages of Scripture (Matt. 12.43, 44; Mark 5.10–14) seem to be in a disembodied state, having existed in some previous period and place in bodily form."[1] He suggests that the disembodied spirits are *from a pre-Adamite race*, but this must remain in the realm of theory, for the suggestion has no Scriptural support.

Dr. Chafer advances the theme that demons were probably created as subjects of Satan in his original angelic glory. Then when Satan fell, he drew them after him (John 8.44; II Pet. 2.4; Jude 6). This hypothesis is known as the *"fallen angel theory"*, and it divides the fallen angels into two classes; those that are free and those that are bound. The free are the demons, while the bound are those angels guilty of such enormous wickedness that they are confined to pits of darkness awaiting judgment (II Pet. 2.4; Jude 6).

The picture becomes more confused when equally able teachers affirm that demons resulted from the union between "sons of God" (fallen angels) and daughters of men. This is *"the monstrous offspring of*

[1] *Christian Theology* (E. H. Bancroft), p. 235.

angels and antediluvian women theory". Dr. De Haan is of the opinion that "The sons of God in this passage were none other than fallen angels who caused a supernatural union with the daughters of man, with the resultant birth of these monstrosities."[1] This theory is open to serious doubts that cannot be satisfactorily answered.

These three propositions are the ones most commonly accepted among evangelicals, but the silence of Scripture makes them nothing more than theoretical hypotheses. Others only show how far man can go in absurdity: for example, that demons are the personifications of violent and incurable diseases, or that they are the spirits of the wicked dead as held by the Jewish historian Josephus. Dr. Edersheim says that Jewish tradition accepted that some demons were created on the eve of the first Sabbath, others were the offspring of Eve and male spirits and of Adam with female spirits, while still others were produced by a process of transformation from vipers.[2] One tradition goes so far as to say that they spring from the backbone of those who have not bent in worship!

The best supported theory is that of fallen angels, though Scripture support is too weak to allow for dogmatism.

II. *What are the typical symptoms of demon possession?*

Some of the following symptoms could also indicate insanity, but all have appeared in cases of true devil possession:

[1] *His Majesty the Devil* (M. R. De Haan), p. 17.
[2] *Life and Times of Jesus the Messiah*, Vol. II, app. 13, p. 759–760.

1. Enlarged eyes and a glassy stare:
2. Fear and intense hatred in the eyes and expression:
3. Flatulence and heavy laboured breathing:
4. A voice not apparently emanating from the vocal chords, frequently using a language unknown to the possessed:
5. Abnormal passions seen in such things as the use of vile epithets, drunkenness and sexual vice:
6. These are frequently accompanied by suicidal impulses:
7. The possessed advances towards one with a wild countenance and often threatening gestures calculated to inspire fear, and when they are rebuffed there is a very violent display of temper:
8. The demons are able to impart supernatural strength which—
9. Promotes acts of violence.

These are some of the more common symptoms of present-day demon possession, many of which are parallelled in the Scriptures: e.g. *Acts of violence* ". . . There met him two possessed with devils, . . . exceeding fierce, so that no man might pass by that way" (Matt. 8.28).

Suicidal impulses ". . . For ofttimes he falleth into the fire, and oft into the water . . ." (Matt. 17.15). Also Mark 9.17–27 which is a remarkable account.

Supernatural strength ". . . a man with an unclean spirit, and no man could bind him, no, not with chains" (Mark 5.3. Also Luke 8.29 and Acts 19.16).

Abnormal passions "A certain man, which had devils long time, and ware no clothes, neither abode in any house, but in the tombs . . ." (Luke 8.27).

III. *How can you be sure that what you call possession is anything more than insanity?*

Many symptoms of possession and insanity are common to both, but there is evidence to show that there is a difference between these two states. Red-Plum, after her deliverance, had to be committed to a mental hospital and it would be tempting to think that she had never been possessed but had gone from one phase of insanity to another. But if she had been merely a mental case, how could she have spoken the Malay language so fluently, a language which she had never used nor studied when in her normal state? It is interesting to note that the sorceress who prescribed the magic concoction was a Malay by birth, and so her familiar spirit spoke in Malay. Another feature was while Red-Plum was possessed, the sounds seemed to proceed from her stomach and not from her vocal chords. After hearing her several times, it sounded as if a demon was speaking from the pit of her stomach. As a pastor I have had to counsel a number of people who showed symptoms of insanity, but not once was I conscious of anything but normal speech. Other evidences of Red-Plum's possession appear in the narrative, but one fact needs emphasis: that when the demon was commanded in the name of Jesus to come out, Red-Plum was immediately delivered. In Scripture demons are cast out by a word of command in the name of Jesus, whereas sickness is dealt with in a different way (Luke 9.49; James 5.13–15). Scripture clearly distinguishes between those who are possessed and those who are sick. ". . . They brought unto him all that were diseased and them that were possessed with devils" (Mark 1.32). Dr. Koch says, "Principally in the New Testament defects or diseases are healed, but the possessed are commanded in the name of Jesus."[1] Sickness, however, does seem to accompany or to follow demon possession.

We also find that the possessed manifest a definite hatred to Christ and His servants. Not only can you feel this hatred, as you deal with the demoniac, but can also see it. At times they come at you as if they would like to tear you apart but, being prevented, their frustration is so great that they spit and threaten. Once I heard a demon tell the heathen present to "pick up clubs and bash his brains out." When they were unable to do so even though some tried, the demon became incoherent in its wrath. The insane do not behave like this in our experience. While they may be violent, they show no hatred when we speak about the Lord Jesus Christ.

One final way of distinguishing between demon possession and mental illness is to use I John 4.2, 3, for a possessed person will always deny that Christ has come in the flesh. Dick Hillis says—"In the cases we handled, if there was any question about whether it was demon possession or a mental case we would use I John 4.2, 3."[2]

IV. *What are the conditions that need be met before a demoniac can be delivered?*

The conditions listed are limited to what we have experienced and know to be true. Both the counsellor

---

[1] *Between Christ and Satan*, p. 30.
[2] *Demon Experiences in Many Lands*, p. 40.

and the sufferer must fulfil certain conditions. It hardly needs to be said that *the counsellor must be a child of God*. Without this union it can be positively dangerous to tangle with demons. Witness the case of the exorcists in the days of Paul (Acts 19.13–16), who, when they attempted to drive out demons in Jesus' name without the proper union, were given a severe buffeting.

There also *needs to be a cleansed heart*. "If I regard iniquity in my heart, the Lord will not hear me" (Ps. 66.18). Demons are intelligent beings and know the history of man. If there is any unconfessed sin in the life, one is powerless and may be embarrassed if the demon exposes the unconfessed sin. "Once a hypocrite from a nearby town came to visit him (the demoniac) and started reading Scripture in an ostentatious way. Fernando made fun of him and asked where he had been the night before."[1] With a cleansed heart it is impossible for the demon to make accusation. ". . . for the prince of this world cometh, and hath nothing in me" (John 14.30).

A strong faith is another requisite—the faith that may lose a minor skirmish, but claims all the promises of God and knows that victory is sure. Lack of faith brings defeat. ". . . Why could not we cast him out? And Jesus said unto them, Because of your unbelief . . ." (Matt. 17.19, 20).

The counsellor *needs to be fearless*. The fearful heart goes hand in hand with unbelief. A strong faith gives a courage which the demon respects. A weak faith produces fear, which the demons recognize and take advantage of. "Why are ye so fearful? how is it that

[1] *Demon Experiences in Many Lands*, p. 51.

ye have no faith?" (Mark 4.40). "Because of the acts of
Christ on the Cross and on Easter morning, counselling
with occultly subjected people is victorious counselling
without fear. Satan and all his cohorts are a defeated
army. All occult powers are made powerless by Jesus."[1]

The counsellor often has to *persevere in prayer and
fasting* before victory is realized. "And he said unto
them, This kind can come forth by nothing, but by
prayer and fasting" (Mark 9.29).

On the part of the demoniac there must be *a
complete surrender to Jesus* without reservation. We
have experienced a number of defeats in our encounters
with evil spirits and have come to the conclusion that
victory is impossible unless there is a complete break
with idolatry and severance with Satan's agents, the
sorcerers. When the family conceals a clinging to
idolatry, the demons will not leave. "No man can
serve two masters . . ." (Matt. 6.24). All the gods,
ancestral shrines, charms, and even the paper on the
wall associated with idol worship must be destroyed.
Only when this has been done can the next step
be taken—namely, the recognition, confession and
putting away of the sin that was the original cause of
the possession. This sin is not always recognized and
needs to be carefully elicited from among a wide
range of human sinfulness, complicated by the
immorality of the heathen. Demons do not take
possession at random but some sin committed (usually
some outrageous act) opens the door for possession.
In West Borneo we have observed that three forms of
sin constitute an invitation to the demon to have

[1] *Between Christ and Satan*, p. 159–160.

possession. Idolatry is the first, for idolatry is the sin of rebellion against the revealed way of worshipping God. "There shall no strange god be in thee; neither shalt thou worship any strange god" (Ps. 81.9, cf. Deut. 13.6–11). Possession often takes place just when the idolater is consorting with sorcerers, worshipping ancestors or partaking of medicine prescribed by the witch doctors. As soon as these forms of idolatry are recognized as the specific grounds for possession, there must be an immediate and complete rejection of them.

A second ground for demon possession is the sins of fornication and adultery (Lev. 20.10; Eph. 5.3). No other sins have caused so much grief to the human race as these. Is it any wonder that the powers of evil use these as a wedge to enter the body of those who sell themselves to these evils? At least two of the cases of possession known to us were the result of sexual offences.

In the case of Mrs. Lo (chapter 10) it was a violent outburst of temper combined with cursing that brought on her bout with demons. There is a strong probability that drunkenness and drug addiction also open the door for the entrance of demons. When the sufferer confesses and forsakes his sin his deliverance is permanent, although he needs to be on guard lest the expelled demons return (Luke 11.24–26). Praise God, where there is confession and a putting away, there are no hopeless cases, for "where sin abounded, grace did much more abound" (Rom. 5.20).

V. *What is the difference between being possessed, oppressed and obsessed by the Devil?*

In *possession* there is a distinct other personality

within and controlling the possessed—a positive invasion by spirit beings of the inner shrine to seize and
subject the whole body and personality: ". . . and they,
entering in, dwelt again in the man" (Matt. 12.45);
"And Jesus asked him saying, What is thy name?
And he said, Legion: because many devils were
entered into him" (Luke 8.30).

Being *oppressed* of the Devil describes a positive
outward attack on the human body by evil spirits to
annoy and to injure. Thus Job was smitten with sore
boils (Job 2.7); the woman with an infirmity was
bound eighteen years by Satan (Luke 13.11, 16); and
Paul given a thorn in the flesh by a messenger of Satan
to buffet him (II Cor. 12.7). Mrs. Needham says "It
has always been the primary object to annoy and
injure the bodies of men."[1]

Being *obsessed* is in a large measure the same as being
influenced by demonic powers, an outward pressure
on man by evil spirits through suggestion and temptation. Thus Satan is able to tempt man with evil
thoughts (I Cor. 7.5); seduces some from Christ by
pleasure (I Tim. 5.11, 15); makes shipwreck of man's
faith (I Tim. 1.19, 20); tempts man to hypocrisy and
lying (Acts 5.3); and causes man to give heed to
doctrines of devils (I Tim. 4.1).

Demons are often able to influence people to do odd,
impetuous, foolish and indecent things. They also
cause abnormal impulses leading to suicide, fits of
temper and inordinate desires for intoxicating bever-
ages, drugs, etc.

Whether it is possession, obsession or oppression, the

[1] *Angels and Demons*, p. 75.

purpose of Satan is the same. His all-consuming and continuing purpose is a rebellion and opposition to the programme of God, and the extension of his own authority as "god" of this world.

VI. *Can anyone be delivered from demon power apart from deliverance through Christ?*

Scripture records that there were professional Jewish exorcists who practised exorcism (Acts 19.13). In the case of the "vagabond Jews" there was complete failure, because they used the name of Jesus in a magical way but lacked faith in the Lord Jesus Christ.

From ancient times, heathen exorcism has depended on mystic incantations and magical ceremonies contrived by Satan to further his work of deception. Mention was made in the chapter on sorcery of the fact that when a sorcerer's familiar spirit holds high office in the spirit domain, that spirit is able to control lesser spirits. In that particular case, by the sorcerer's use of mystic incantations, the familiar spirit was able to drive away the lesser spirit. But there was no permanent deliverance in that case.

I have also witnessed another phenomenon that has caused me much exercise of thought. In West Borneo there are sorcerers who have completely lost their powers as a medium after leaving their own sphere of influence, only to recover them upon return. I have also known a lad declared insane and sent to a distant hospital for treatment. Before the doctor could commence shock treatment the patient became completely normal. So long as he stayed in that district he remained normal, but when he later returned home for a visit, he immediately became violent and had to be chained, which suggests demon possession rather than insanity. When he crossed an invisible boundary he was delivered, but when he returned he became possessed once more. Scripture contains only a suggestion of this, but experience points to the fact that some demons are forbidden to leave their assigned areas. Thus when the possessed leave the area assigned to the demon, the demon has to leave his victim.

Despite these facts I firmly believe that while possessed persons may be helped and even temporarily delivered, they can experience no permanent deliverance except through Christ. Matt. 12.43–45 speaks of an unclean spirit that had left an individual for a season, only to return at a later date bringing with it "seven other spirits more wicked than himself: and the last state of that man is worse than the first." Christ cast out devils "with the finger of God" (Luke 11.20), and that power is vested in all of His disciples Luke 10.17).

VII. *Is it always wilful sin that causes demon possession?*

While grounds for possession are the yielding to some outrageous sin against God or mankind, it is true that, while the heathen may know the act he is committing is wrong, he does not always realize that it is a sin against God. Therefore, the question of wilful sin concerns only the believer.

Whenever the possibility of a believer being possessed is mentioned, an immediate reaction against the idea is usual. Dr. Unger says, "To demon possession only unbelievers are exposed; to demon influence, both believers and unbelievers".[1] He reasons that a believer who is sealed, indwelt and filled by the Holy Spirit is not susceptible to demon inhabitation. This is a powerful argument, but an interpretation of three passages of Scripture might modify this view. They are I Cor. 5.5, "To deliver such an one unto Satan for the destruction of the flesh, that the spirit may be saved in the day of the Lord Jesus"; "Whom I have delivered unto Satan, that they may learn not to blaspheme" (I Tim. 1.20); and "that they may recover themselves out of the snare of the devil, who are taken captive by him at his will" (II Tim. 2.26).

If for some gross sin God authorizes the Church to hand over the believer again to the bondage of Satan for chastisement, is it unreasonable to believe that while under this bondage the believer is liable not only to demon influence and oppression, but to possession as well? The Rev. J. A. MacMillan says "The reality and possibility of children of God falling under the power of the enemy and finding themselves controlled by him is a tremendous reality."[2] He also cites several illustrations of *believers* being delivered from demon possession.

Much as we would like to think it impossible for believers to be possessed, evidence has accumulated to suggest that it is a distinct possibility. We have observed one case in West Borneo where a believer was re-possessed because of a sin she committed after she had been delivered.

To the question, "Is it a wilful sin that brings on

[1] *Biblical Demonology*, p. 100.
[2] *Modern Demon Possession*, p. 35.

possession?" the answer is a positive "yes". When a believer is guilty of deliberate immorality or gross sin, he is liable to demon possession. It is also possible for a believer to lay himself open to an invasion of evil spirits when he abandons himself to the seeking of spiritual gifts and manifestations without understanding the manner in which the Holy Spirit bestows spiritual gifts. In so doing, he yields his body up passively to supernatural powers.

VIII. *Does a person always know when he is demon possessed?*

This depends on the type of possession. The person who consents to be the medium of a familiar spirit always knows when the spirit manifests itself. This is voluntary possession. In cases of involuntary possession where some ground has been given for possession, there may or may not be a knowledge of the demon's presence. This has been borne out in our experience with those who have been set free from demonic power.

But there is also the type of possession where the demons bury themselves in the human personality without the knowledge of the one they possess. The demons sometimes affect the organs of the body, sometimes the intellect, and sometimes the spiritual nature of man. In this case they can be classified as the "angels of light" demons, who counterfeit the real ministry of the Holy Spirit in the life of the Christian. Dr. Chafer says, "Demon possession in the present time is probably often unsuspected because of the generally unrecognized fact that demons are capable of inspiring a moral and exemplary life, as well as of appearing as the dominating spirit of a spiritist medium."[1]

IX. *If the God we worship is so powerful that we can cast out demons in His name, why don't we seek out the many possessed and deliver them?*

First and foremost because we have no record of Jesus and His disciples seeking out the demon possessed to deliver them. The general Scripture pattern is described in the words "And *they brought* unto Him all sick people that were taken with divers diseases and torments, and those which were possessed with devils . . ." (Matt. 4.24). The possessed were all brought to Jesus in a voluntary way. When Jesus sent out His disciples to evangelize (Luke 9.1-6), power and authority were given to heal and cast out demons, but this was merely secondary to their preaching ministry. The natural results of preaching is a search for healing for the suffering body.

Another reason for not seeking out the demon possessed is that it is impossible to help them unless they desire it. If the possessed is in such a condition that he is beyond this desire, it is then up to the relatives to take the initiative. But avarice usually makes heathen relatives unwilling to meet the conditions needed to bring about a deliverance.

X. *What is an apparition?*

It is a ghostly materialization by spirit beings of a material and bodily form. These materializations

[1] *Satan* (Lewis Sperry Chafer), p. 68.

apparently appear to man for both good and evil reasons. Chapter 7 tells how Chrysanthemum was helped by an apparition for good purposes and chapter 5 records how another woman experienced nightly appearances of evil apparitions for malevolent purposes. The Christian members of the family never actually saw the apparition, but could feel the presence of the evil thing.

Scripture records how God prevented the king of Syria from harming Elisha by causing the appearance of a large spectral army (II Kings 6.8–23). God sends His angels as "ministering spirits" and sometimes they do actually become visible for the purpose of protecting the child of God (Heb. 1.14; Ps. 34.7; 91.11).

On the other hand, demons seem to have the power to make appearances and give visions in order to harass mankind. There was once a fatal bus accident in West Borneo which the bus driver and several passengers attributed to the sudden appearance of a spectral being in the path of the vehicle, causing the bus driver to swerve in an attempt to avoid it. The bus crashed and two passengers were killed.

Both Scripture and experience attest to the reality of ghostly apparitions.

CHAPTER FOURTEEN

LIVING VICTORIOUSLY

"Thine, O Lord, is the victory" (I Chron. 29.11).

THE LORD JESUS on the day of His betrayal and death called the exercise of Satan's power, "the power of darkness" (Luke 22.53). Elsewhere Scripture warns against the rulers of darkness (Eph. 6.12), and the working of Satan (II Thess. 2.9). We are also warned to have "no fellowship with the unfruitful works of darkness but rather reprove them" (Eph. 5.11). The Bible describes Satan as a prince of darkness, that is, a prince over a highly organized kingdom of darkness, resolute in its opposition to God and His kingdom of light (II Cor. 4.4; Eph. 6.12; I John 5.1; Acts 26.18). Many other Scriptures confirming this deserve careful study.

One only needs to read the newspaper, turn on the T.V. or radio to be made aware of the devilment in the world today. John declares that "The whole world lieth in wickedness" (I John 5.19). The Bible nowhere promises that world conditions will improve, but rather that they will "wax worse and worse, deceiving and being deceived" (II Tim. 3.13). In the days in which we now live, innumerable evil forces are in a frenzy of activity, knowing that their time is short (Rev. 20.2). Led by the arch-enemy of God and man's soul, they spare no effort to bring man down to the same level of their depravity. Consider the following statements:

". . . that old serpent, called the Devil, and Satan which deceiveth the whole world" (Rev. 12.9).

". . . Lest by some means the tempter have tempted you . . ." (I Thess. 3.5).

". . . after the working of Satan with all power and signs and lying wonders, and with all deceivableness of unrighteousness . . ." (II Thess. 2.9–10).

". . . The snare of the devil" (I Tim. 3.7).

". . . unfruitful works of darkness, . . ." (Eph. 5.11).

"In the latter times some shall depart from the faith, giving heed to seducing spirits, and doctrines of devils" (I Tim. 4.1).

Many Scriptures seem to imply that men who reject the Lord or who are disobedient to His Word come under the control of these seducing spirits who do everything in their power to darken the foolish heart of man. The Christian who wonders why he is defeated in his life and testimony should note the words of Jesus to Peter, ". . . Behold, Satan hath desired to have you, that he may sift you as wheat" (Luke 22.31). It is a tragic fact that Satan still finds a way to defeat us despite the fact that Christ has given us every weapon necessary for the defeat of the Enemy; but we have failed to make use of them.

Years ago on my mother's knee I was taught a little verse that I have never forgotten:

> If he can't get in at the window,
> He'll try to come in at the door,
> Or through the skylight, in the dead of the night;
> Or else he'll come in at the floor.
> But I have a Friend who will keep him out, . . .

Praise God, the picture is not all dark for a light

shines into the darkness! We have been delivered out of the authority of darkness by the mighty act of Jesus at Calvary (Col. 1.13). In the miracle of the new birth and of the indwelling Christ, every provision has been made for victory over the foe. It is only when the believer explicitly disobeys God's Word that he can be defeated. "Resist the devil" (James 4.7) is no idle injunction. When the believer self-confidently relies on his own ability to contend with the foe, he leaves himself open to defeat and subsequent discouragement. A knowledge of Satan as the "god of this world" (II Cor. 4.4) must make us flee to the "Rock" and refuse to do battle in our own strength.

"What would you do if Satan should knock at your heart's door?" a twelve-year-old girl was asked.

"Teacher, I would not answer Satan's knock, but just send Jesus to the door"—a truth many Christians take years to learn. Did not Moses say to God's people, ". . . Stand still, and see the salvation of the Lord" (Ex. 14.13)? We experience defeat when we try to meet the Enemy in our own strength. But when we stand still in the face of temptation and let the Captain of our salvation, the Lord Jesus Christ, battle with the enemy, then, and only then, does the Devil flee from us.

Why, then, should the Christian live in a state of despondency, knowing no victory over the world, the flesh and the Devil? If we have indeed been delivered from the power of darkness, why is it so hard to become victorious Christians? If God has provided the weapons for victory, why haven't we appropriated them?

Is it not because we have accepted Him only as Lord of our salvation, and not as Lord of our lives? There must be a new and continuous awakening to the meaning of "Christ in you, the hope of glory" (Col. 1.27). Until this is realized, there can be no hope of victory. Satan has had too many years to practise his devices for mere humans to conquer him in their own strength. But listen to the words of Jesus when He says, "*I in them*, and thou in me, that they may be made perfect in one;" and again, "And I have declared unto them thy name, and will declare it: that the love wherewith thou hast loved me may be in them, *and I in them*" (John 17.23, 26).

Lamenting past failures will not help, but a continuous, daily recognition that Christ indwells us and is sufficient for every need will give us the strength and courage to stand against the wiles of the Devil. This truth is not easily grasped and some go right through life without learning it. Nevertheless it is clearly taught in Scripture, and my prayer is that others may experience the joy that was mine on the day when the truth was driven home to my heart. I would never have had the courage to write of my encounters with demonic activity without the knowledge of the Indwelling One.

Many truths in the Word of God are a source of strength in our warfare against the Devil, but the realization of the indwelling Christ, and a day by day acknowledgment, acceptance and utilization of this truth, will set us on the victory road and keep us there. Christ has never been, and can never be defeated by Satan. How is it then that we are so often defeated and give way to discouragement and despondency? We are not left without an answer to that problem in Scripture.

"God . . . even when we were dead in sins, hath quickened us together with Christ . . . and hath raised us up together, and made us sit together in heavenly places in Christ Jesus" (Eph. 2.4–6) reveals that our authority to defeat the works of darkness is the inherent right of the child of God. Being identified with Christ we share all the authority that Christ has (Eph. 1.19). Paul says, "I can do all things through Christ which strengtheneth me" (Phil. 4.13).

Christians, whatever their need or problem, need only claim their position in Christ, accept their throne rights and see Satan go down, a defeated foe! Taking the shield of faith, we shall be able to quench all the fiery darts of the wicked (Eph. 6.16).

"A faith in what?" A faith in the indwelling Christ, who "having spoiled principalities and powers, . . . made a shew of them openly, triumphing over them in it" (Col. 2.15): a faith in the knowledge that the "Son of God was manifested, that he might destroy the works of the devil" (I John 3.8); a faith that all the authority Christ has, and His power to overcome all forces of evil is our inherent right given to us by Almighty God. We stand on Ephesians 1.19.

Scripture makes it plain that we have the power to overcome the Enemy, but is that enough? No, positively not. We must *put on* the *whole* armour of God (Eph. 6.11–18). Our fight is not against human power, but against the rulers of darkness. No one goes into battle without being armed, or defeat will surely follow. Daily we must put on every single piece of armour God has provided for us.

Ephesians reveals another secret of victory. "Neither give place to the devil" (Eph. 4.27). If the Christian harbours sin in his life, he gives Satan a foothold from which he cannot be dislodged until all is made right. It behoves us, then, to be watchful. So-called "little sins" have a way of creeping into our lives and with them the opportunity for Satan to gain a victory. Peter also says, "Be sober, be vigilant; because your adversary the devil . . . walketh about, seeking whom he may devour" (I Pet. 5.8).

Finally, when James says, "Resist the devil, and he will flee from you" (James 4.7), he does not mean that we are to resist him in our own strength. Resistance in God's strength is implied, for the beginning of verse 7 reads "Submit yourselves therefore to God". The secret of living victoriously is in our submission to God, for in submitting, we acknowledge Him as Lord of our life and pledge ourselves to be obedient, trusting and faithful servants. As we yield to God's almighty direction, we enjoy complete protection and immunity against the assaults of the crafty agents of evil.

Accepting this God-provided provision, let us go forth to battle knowing that "If God be for us, who can be against us?" (cf. I Chron. 29.11).

"Thanks be unto God, which always causeth us to triumph in Christ" (II Cor. 2.14).

". . . Thanks be to God, which giveth us the victory through our Lord Jesus Christ" (I Cor. 15.57).

EPILOGUE

THIS BOOK MAKES no claim to be a complete treatise on demonology. Its matter is controversial, for there has always been a difference of opinion on this subject. But if the believer is awakened to the peril surrounding him and to a more careful study of the devices of Satan in the Scriptures so that he may better fight the good fight of faith, the author's purpose will have been fulfilled.

BIBLIOGRAPHY

BANCROFT, E. H. *Christian Theology*.

CHAFER, L. S. *Satan*, new and revised edition, Moody Press, Chicago.

DE HAAN, M. R. *His Majesty the Devil*, Bible Class, Grand Rapids.

EDERSHEIM, A. *Life and Times of Jesus the Messiah*, Vol. II, Longmans, Green & Co., New York, 1940.

HILLIS, R. *Demon Experiences in Many Lands*, Colportage Library 427, Moody Press, Chicago, 1960.

HOULISTON, S. *Borneo Breakthrough*, Overseas Missionary Fellowship, London.

IRVINE, W. C. *Heresies Exposed*, 11th edition, Loizeaux Bros., New York, 1940.

KOCH, K. E. *Between Christ and Satan*, Berghausen Bd., Evangelization Publishers (Germany), 1961.

LEWIS, C. S. *The Screwtape Letters*, Geoffrey Bles, London.

MACMILLAN, J. A. *Modern Demon Possession*, Christian Publications Inc., Harrisburg.

NEEDHAM, MRS. G. C. *Angels and Demons*, Colportage Library 292, Moody Press, Chicago.

PENN-LEWIS, MRS., and ROBERTS, E. *War on the Saints*, Marshall Brothers, London, 1912.

— *War on the Saints* (abridged edition), The Overcomer Literature Trust, Parkstone, 1956.

SAUER, E. *From Eternity to Eternity*, Paternoster Press, Exeter.

UNGER, M. R. *Biblical Demonology*, 3rd edition, Scripture Press, Chicago, 1955.